Seek the Secret Code
of the Universe

A Testament from Charmie Gilcrease, the beautiful Kriyaban who themed the two volumes of quotes.

Here is a quote from Yogacharya David that especially speaks to my heart right now. Although this quote isn't from me, it is me.

"Though I made uncountable mistakes, somehow God and Guru never let go of me, though I let go of them. Due to this grace, I learned, changed, and became something new; yet it is a state of consciousness that is deeply familiar—as if it has always been true, always been me. My old life is now seen as something long ago; it is as if I have lived many lives in this one lifespan, some of them almost unrecognizable as being me."

About Yogacharya David

"What can I say about David? I met him when I was 19 and very new on the path this life. He was a long-haired 'hippy' type and rather acerbic in speech. He intrigued and puzzled me. With Mother, I was so in awe I could barely speak around her and could only see the great shining God Self within her. With David, I was able to perceive the human self become the God Self and that experience was a guiding star. Knowing that I, myself, could become my God Self wasn't impossible—hard, but not impossible. Yogacharya David set a wonderful example for many of us."

—Charmie Gilcrease

Seek the Sacred Code
of the Universe
Quotes: Volume Two

Yogacharya David R. Hickenbottom

Editor: Ruth M. Lamb, Ph.D

The Cross and The Lotus Publishing
Camano Island, Washington, USA

For permission requests, contact the publisher at:
http://www.crossandlotus.com/contact.html

ISBN: 978-1-957811-18-5 (softcover)
ISBN: 978-1-957811-19-2 (eBook)

All photos courtesy of Carla Hickenbottom Portfolio

Edited by Ruth Lamb

Book design by Jan Westendorp, katodesignandphoto.com

Cover design by Rob Landers, Ruth Lamb, and Jan Westendorp

Printed and bound in Canada by Digital Direct Printing, Victoria, BC

Published by
The Cross and The Lotus Publishing
Camano Island, Washington, USA
Website: www.crossandlotus.com

Contents

Preface

Yogacharya David (1954–2019), a western man who sought to discover the sacred that lies behind the five senses and materialism, was drawn to his Guru, Mother Hamilton, and his life underwent an evolutionary change. He discovered the grandeur and challenges presented when seeking the highest, most loving Truth: a Truth that is within, behind, in front, beneath, and above our daily existence.

Seeking the highest truth consciousness, Yogacharya David discovered his Self, or soul—his unique sovereign integral connection with the Divine Source or Spirit. After many years of dedicated outer and inner work that purifies and attunes the physical, emotional, spiritual, and etheric bodies, he achieved self-realization: an inner connection with Divine Grace as it lives through his unique presence on this beautiful planet.

Through the years, Yogacharya David gave over 1000 talks to devotees, wrote in journals, composed poems, and developed a series of discourses and other writings.

His teachings are now presented in books. An outline of those published to date is at the end of this book.

Resurrect the Listening Heart and Mind: Quotes Volume One and this volume, titled *Seek the Sacred Code of the Universe: Quotes Volume Two,* consist of quotes selected from Yogacharya David's six volume discourse series written between 2013 and 2019. Major themes in Quotes volume two are Dharma, Love and Truth, Who is Our Self? and, Will and Surrender.

Short and replete with wisdom: each discourse is a gem. The quotes chosen here are but a small selection designed to provide upliftment in the moment—a quick reference to start or end a day, or to be a guide during reflective or arduous moments. Significantly, if you receive the words with your heart, you will be able to receive the higher consciousness through the frequency of Yogacharya David's words.

Enjoy.

OM TAT SAT AUM

Introduction

POEM

Spirit Calls

I soar upon wings of bliss;
Circumference never,
Open, clear, expansive, and joyful—
Oh, what remarkable freedom is mine!
It is the bliss long-sought, a freedom hard-won.
How many years in the making?
How many tears shed in sorrow?
Only to discover the keys to freedom
Were in my hands all the time!
Now I soar and soar and soar,
Sometimes my feet touch the ground,
Other times I am borne in the air—
No tethers, no gravity, and no limits.
Whether of the earth or the air
I serve the Infinite One—and with fire He scorches,
Removing ignorance from this world.
Dear ones, let us soar together;
Successfully fighting with worldly-gravity that binds,
And be as one with our infinite Beloved.
For even now, the Song of Spirits is calling to us all.[1]

---

1   Yogacharya David, *Climbing the Sacred Mountain: Poems and Prayers of a Western Yogi* (p. 285).

SEEK THE
SACRED CODE OF
THE UNIVERSE

Yogacharya David, Maple Ridge, BC, 2011.

Dharma

GROWING INWARD

Sadhana—your practice of God-remembrance—must permeate every part of your life for the total transformation in divinizing your life. God-remembrance takes place in your deeper meditations, when you divinely love on a spring-filled day; when you are at home doing your daily chores, watching a movie, in conversation with friends, driving your car, at work, or in your private musings.

―――∞∞∞―――

Begin today by transferring your allegiance, your focus of attention, and your love, to God and not the world. You will still live in the world. Therefore, you must give it its due. However, inwardly, deeply, you look to God as your all and all, in all. Discover that amazingly, simply, your heart's desire and fulfillment is, and always has been, right within you.

―――∞∞∞―――

There are advanced stages of meditation in which consciousness effortlessly synchronizes with any one of the three bodies—physical, astral, causal—or beyond.

―――∞∞∞―――

An observation: as a guest in someplace new, in particular one of nature's cathedrals, there is a depth of experience that can be had by the sensitive soul. To get this depth you must have a certain attunement to the subtle world that resides just behind this gross material one. I have observed that the majority of people who tour a new place are engaged in conversation with others about times and places other than where they are at. Such a preoccupation excludes the more subtle plane of inner experience. To feel the soul of a place, or the lack of it, to be aware of the spirit that may be present one must be focused in the present and open to this inner awareness.

※

Immersing yourself into the Bliss and Light of God is at the heart of every aspirant.

※

Do not let your mind limit you to the possibilities of what you may be as you grow in Christ-Consciousness. You are a child of the Infinite, and as such you are made in His likeness and image.

※

First, make daily contact with the God within through your deepened communion with the Infinite Spirit. Then mindfully enter into this world of activity by expressing joy, peace, and bliss; letting these qualities saturate your thoughts and words and guide your activities.

All time and space are filled with sacred vibration, so live life fully and be an instrument of Spirit at all times and in all places.

I choose God, I choose empowerment of choice for healthy habits, I choose love, and I choose to continue to learn, grow, serve, and to be happy!

If you have not yet realized God fully, it means you are harboring fear and/or anger that does not allow you to experience this surpassingly beautiful peace. Expose your innermost workings before God, surrender all that you knowingly or unknowingly are keeping for yourself, then lay it all at the feet of your infinite Beloved. Experience His peace as never before, then you will go on to be a Light unto this world.

The power of pristine nature is undeniable; however, it should not be seen in lieu of the power of the life-force that is unleashed in the Son of man, the human form; rather, nature may be seen as an adjunctive help. Spiritual forces within the spine and brain are of unparalleled dimensions.

The way through temptation is to keep your mind upon God. The qualities you will experience when in tune with God will be quite different from those experienced when you are in ignorance.

In the light you will be calm, clear, humble, not driven by lower forces; you can easily stand in the light in humble submission and will not turn away.

—∽∾∾∽—

For the spiritual aspirant to find balance in this world is a great art.

—∽∾∾∽—

You only need to keep with your practice, remain receptive, and the yeast of the God-seed within you will find the right conditions to grow, flower, bear fruit, and ripen into full God-experience.

The God-seed is not far away or in some distant time, but within easy range of your inward mind.

—∽∾∾∽—

Replacing "no, I can't" consciousness with "yes, I will" consciousness is a tremendous step in evolution.

—∽∾∾∽—

The only way to the deeper truth of any subject is through refined intuition. Certainly, the reasoning mind plays an important role in gathering information and performing analysis, but that part of the brain can never ascertain absolute higher meaning. For that truth is known in deeper states of meditation which open a doorway to greater reality.

Let us put the universal truths we do know to work; not delay even a moment. Meditation is a keystone, for it is in turning the mind inward that we touch the hem of God, and through that proximity, we are purified and these universal truths then spontaneously live themselves through us. Thus, we find confirmed through our own experience, that those truths we have sensed for so long are directly revealed by the Author of all life—and are freshly born in us.

Think also of accomplishing what you have come to do in this world: service to humanity and the fulfillment of your dreams. Expand your consciousness to comfortably and easily accommodate your dreams—definitely invite God in to be co-creator with you.

Remember, you are made in His likeness and His image; there are no limits to what He can do through you.

The vast majority of people are focused on the solid-material nature of this world, some see the fluid-like movement of life-energy in and around things and people, and a few have the vision to see what cannot be seen by others, the thought-trons (Master's terminology) behind all that is—a causal realm that is much larger and more profound than all other aspects of creation.

We look about us and see the crystalized life-energy of this world, but there is so much more that is not visible to the naked eye. The three aspects of creation can be polluted just like water . . . The material, energetic, and idea realms can become toxic and manifests as disease and darkness of every description: an energy of darkness may form around someone depressed: the mind may become filled with wicked thoughts, or the body may suffer due to past wrong actions.

———

Jesus gave us the great commandment to put God first, then everything else (according to His will) will be added to our life. However, the human ego does this in reverse, it seeks out the world, and then gives burnt offerings (used up life-force) to God, if anything at all.

———

The more we explore the teachings of Jesus the clearer it is what a magnificent Avatar he is. Our teachings are rooted in Jesus and Krishna, and find universal resonance throughout all the world's great religions and spiritual traditions.

Let us use this opportunity to go deeper into silent meditation and be lifted up as on wings of angels in His peace and Divine Presence.

———

Let us pick up our cross, the body, and follow after our Lord, to meditate deeply upon that inner Light that is seeking to draw us unto itself. This story is not a fairy tale, nor is it an event that only took place two thousand years ago, but this is a living legacy from all those who have gone before us into resurrected Divine Consciousness— and is seeking to do so in you now.

———❧———

In themselves material advances do not represent wisdom. These leaps in technology we have seen have certainly made things possible that would have been science fiction not long ago. But—are we happier, more at peace, living in greater harmony with our environment and each other?

———❧———

Material wealth and prestige come and go with the seasons of life. Youth, strength, and health can all fall by the wayside—what is permanent? The only thing that is lasting is our spiritual heritage that we may realize in all its fullness. God made creation with fascinating, never-ending expressions, but all have an expiry date attached.

Only God can fulfill that need we all have for the inner kingdom of heaven, promised from when the foundation of this universe was created. As we celebrate this sacred experience of the resurrection of Christ Consciousness, think deeply upon its meaning, and make a determination that this symbolic teaching will find fulfillment in you.

———❧———

Ahimsa (non-harmfulness) can only come by being established in an unshakable calm; come to the point of spiritual evolution where every thought, word, and action is saturated with the inward flow of God-consciousness.

———— ∞ ————

In a reciprocal manner, right action leads us into greater attunement with higher consciousness. Higher consciousness then becomes a direct guide for right action—as long as the individual remains mindful of both right action and inner attunement, the growth of both makes for a seamless life of wisdom and intuitively guided right action.

———— ∞ ————

In the beginning, when attaining samadhi the body becomes fixed, the breath is still–what can appear to be a death state—however, the soul has never been more fully alive. As purification continues, the aspirant may remain in God-consciousness while moving the body, however there are times of having this unbroken consciousness, and other times feeling separation.

Ultimately the soul, through deepened communion, is able to go about its business in the world without a break—the individual, ever one with the Divine nature of his or her Soul.

———— ∞ ————

Through intelligent application of will with a higher purpose, the aspirant realizes the fullest benefit of transmuted sexual energy. Creating a list of "do-nots" without understanding its tremendous positive potential leads to perversion. However, with a clear awareness of all that sexual energy can do, the ways it is transformed into creative endeavors and spiritual upliftment, the aspirant discovers the real source of a truly liberating sexual revolution.

Blame and shame are two mindsets that inhibit learning. I sometimes joke that to assign blame early and often is a management tool. You see this with some personalities, their default is to blame others. An enormous consequence of doing this is that it engenders feeling powerless.

There is no limit to this transformation. It all starts with those who are responsive to the call of truth and have the courage to seek it out; to know deep within themselves that attaining direct perception of God is their real purpose in life; that all religions are, in reality, here to guide and support those striving for the realization of their eternal being and existence.

Attunement with dharma leads to spiritual freedom, ignoring or going against those principles of ultimate truth leads to wrong actions and further binds the soul in ignorance and darkness.

All those called to the spiritual path are here to awaken to the greater Reality. While we must navigate the waves on the surface of this material reality, our greater task is to explore the immensity below the waves.

——————

The first benefit is that while in God-awareness, you remain in a calm center. Like a skilled athlete you operate in "the zone" where there is a natural flow in body and mind. From that calm center, you are in a prime position to use the reasoning mind as well as the intuitional mind. Like a general observing the field of combat, you see the movement of forces and calculate what needs to be done, not overwhelmed by the noise and confusion of war. This calm reason adds and subtracts based on experience and learning.

The intuitional mind does not add or subtract, at least not consciously—it knows through direct perception what is true. Intuition comes, not through reasoning, but as a flash of insight. Both reason and intuition are invaluable aids for you to operate in this world.

——————

In the beginning, you focus on the third eye and cultivate dispassion for the things of the body and the world. Then you get glimpses into the actual experience where you are aware of this greater reality. Then you pass through the jnani phase where the world is continuously perceived as a dream, and the inner reality is far more real. As body and mind are purified, you gradually enter into the universal vision in which you are aware of the Divine Nature both within and without. Oh, what a transformation this is!

In one sense, your life is outwardly just the same, but inwardly, you are transformed. Life still happens, all of its ups and downs, and the body will still one day decay and die, but you are inwardly free–you are now established in your true Home.

———

These three spiritual bodies—physical, astral, causal—are not merely theoretical, but practical and very real experiences that are known to the advanced spiritual scientist.

———

You think this world is wonderful, and there is no denying it is a marvelous creation, but in comparison with the greatness of God inside of you it is as nothing.

———

Daily I feel the greatness and expansion of God's Spirit. In truth, I know that all who actively attune themselves to God, and God in this form, will receive of this power and light of the Infinite.

———

Because God is beyond cause and effect, you can experience this joy-filled freedom independent of circumstances. And, due to the fact that God is purity itself, the more you focus on God, the better your choices are.

Let us love and strive as bhaktas, discriminate as jnanas, and follow in the steps of great spiritual masters in attaining the universal-vision, becoming para-bhaktas; free in the ultimate realization as the human and the Divine merge. Then, no matter where we look, what we do, there is only One, only God.

When you sit for meditation, take with you your remembrance of your connection with saints and realized masters from the world over; plug into the Creator of all that is. What a sacred privilege this is, and in the depths of your meditation you are fulfilling what you have come to do.

Let human-made limitations arouse your innate spiritual dynamics, a challenge to God to rise up in pre-eminence—a superior Creator to His creation.

PERSEVERENCE

The world is stood on its head. If someone stands for clear values, they are seen as villains, and if someone spits in the eye of core values, they are held up as heroes. There is even less popular culture support for dharma and spiritual living today than at any previous time.

———

It is both in the persistence and the patience that our spiritual life can play such a large roll. Attunement with God brings strength of will to act, along with the faith that doors will open according to His will.

Attunement also gives us patience, for all is ultimately in His hands.

———

It can be said that God has desire when He sets this entire creation into motion. Everywhere about us there is beauty and wonder and awe in beholding what the Creator has accomplished. All evolution of this universe from the coalescence of stars and planets, to the diverse biological species up to humankind, represents a gradual order, splendor, and balance that defies "randomness" of creation.

———

For every slip and fall on the path, you can trace it back to a falloff of intensity in your spiritual practice. If you find that your practice is dry, that temptation or doubt has crept in the back door and made itself home in your mind, then let the alarms sound to awaken you to the fact that the liar and thief have made inroads.

—∞∞∞∞—

Let us attune ourselves to action based on the highest nature. This requires that we be mindful of our thoughts, words, and actions. We know the difference when we are acting out of our highest nature and when we are responding to the demons within. All sincere aspirants will immediately self-correct when temporarily taken over by the seductive devilish nature and re-align with angelic purity and Light.

—∞∞∞∞—

Whether your dharma has you living in a cave or a mansion, whether you are in the humblest or most visible vocation, if it is right for you, then you need not envy anyone in this whole world for you are exactly where your loving Creator has placed you.

At times, it may be a great struggle to get there, but living in your true Self fulfills all of your heart's desires today, from moment to moment.

—∞∞∞∞—

Beauty can grow in the most terrible conditions. In fact, the reason that some plants stand out is that their situation is so forbidding.

—∞∞∞∞—

We find in Arjuna exactly the right attitude in life. This world is a battlefield of competing interests; to run away leaves the field to those who are driven by lower desires. If good people do not become policemen, then those posts are left to scoundrels and the world suffers. This is true of all positions, from the janitor to CEOs of large companies, political leaders, and spiritual ministers.

Dharma, right action, betters the world, adharma, wrong motives, brings suffering.

Like all great principles, they are not the property of any one person, religion, or nation—they are universal and equally true for one and for all. We can draw inspiration from the idealism and courage of those who succeeded against all the odds in bringing forward a nation based on the ideals: "We hold these truths to be self-evident, that all men are created equal by their Creator with certain inalienable Rights, that among these are Life, Liberty and the Pursuit of Happiness. That to secure these rights, Governments are instituted among Men, deriving their just powers from the consent of the governed." [2]

Due to human fallibility, there may be those who doubt divine inspiration for this country, but that has always been the case with sacred ideals—as God proposes, it is up to human beings to fulfill His high ideals. Imperfect implementation does not mean that it does not come

---

2   From the *United States Declaration of Independence*.
https://www.archives.gov

from the most perfect One; only that we need to work harder to be on God's side.

———∞∞∞———

We have been given the keys to the kingdom of heavenly happiness. We have also been given the choice as to whether to use those keys or to carry on the old patterns of misery-producing habits.

We hold the keys in our own hands for finding the eternal lightness of Being radiating in the deepest recesses of our Self. However, only if we mindfully use those keys will we find the source of eternal life—those *Living Waters* make us know that eternal life is the true nature of our Soul, and is discovered through intensified prayer and meditation.

These vital energies may also lead to a long life and youthfulness of the body as well, but what of that if Self-realization is not attained?

———∞∞∞———

To love God is not simply a duty—something we must do. It is the greatest thing we can do for ourselves and for the world! Opening our heart to God is a choice, but in the beginning, it is not an easy one. We have all been hurt and have met with disappointment when it comes to loving others; however, in loving God, we have a beloved who will never hurt or betray us: He is as steady and constant as we are to Him—not that God ever turns away from us, but He will never intrude upon us if the door of our heart is closed.

Just as in marriage: in good times and bad, sickness and in health, in prosperity or adversity, beloved I am ever yours. That is our vow, our commitment, and we keep it unconditionally in our marriage with God. He is our eternal Beloved, and though He might be able to do without us, we could not exist for even a nano-second without Him.

This human love, whether in romance, friendship, work, or familial relationships, is all preparation for our marriage with God. God is the consummate lover, ever attentive, giving, and keen for our welfare. However, even as God gives all, so does He demand all. The principle of, "As you give, so shall you receive," is never truer than with God.

A human tendency is to withhold from another when hurt and disappointed. This tendency must be overcome, not only in human relationships (this is part of the preparation for the Divine Romance), but most especially, you must learn not to withhold from God. There is a mathematical preciseness—exactly the way you withhold equals blocking out the flow of God; not because God is withholding from you, but because you have built a barrier through your withholding.

The preexistent soul is free of desire nature and common human needs—it is of pure light and consciousness. When soul consciousness mingles with earthly expression, it can be done with a light touch—producing no binding attachments. However, the soul can also become focused on the object of the senses, creating a desire for more and more.

This desire nature creates a split of the human self from the real Self.

Now, instead of being a pure Soul-expression, awareness is driven by desire nature. Sex, along with survival instinct, and desire for power are incredible allurements that are occasionally satisfied, but always call for more. Consciousness, controlled by these forces, falling from its original state of freedom, is now at the beck and call of lower impulses. Sexual energy being so powerful, and having such a drawing power, becomes binding when unregulated in human affairs—it literally and symbolically is the counter-opposite of spiritual freedom.

On the way to an exalted state of awareness, we stand with feet in two worlds; one foot in the material existence, the other in the awareness of God's presence. In this sometimes tenuous, in-between state, we must demonstrate the utmost integrity—not sliding into forgetfulness of Divine awareness.

Know that in seeking out God first, it is also for the highest good of the world. However, the world oftentimes does not share that view; so, it makes its demands on us. In the process, we must choose—situation by situation; we are tested to put God first.

We are richly privileged to be living this spiritual life, with the highest teachings and the greatest examples of fully realized masters to guide our way. And in living this life we are each day tested to put God first, to love Him most.

Let us ever keep this lofty goal uppermost in mind, tread this path with firm steps, never wavering, or faltering. The greatest happiness and spiritual wealth are with us now—it is our greatest treasure imaginable.

—⁂—

Every life has a unique set of circumstances for what a soul has come to learn. It is incumbent upon you to be clear as to what is essential for you to learn and to become.

You must be fully aware of what is important to you, and to align the mechanics of your life to support those important and essential goals. Through this alignment, you may rightfully enjoy peace and an absolutely fulfilled life.

—⁂—

The Galilean Master said you cannot serve two masters; you must choose—either serve God or the world.

You definitely live in this world, and you must render unto Caesar what is Caesar's; however, there should never be a doubt about who your true master is—who is central to your heart, mind, and soul, and who it is that you are truly serving.

—⁂—

There must be a foundation, firm principles on which to build our spiritual practice: tenets that can lead us to freedom and not into further bondage to the ego, to the things of the senses, and this world.

———

The word resurrection has interesting Latin roots. It comes from the verb rego, to make straight, plus the preposition of sub, or under; then surrectum, to rise. Put together, it is "a straightening from under again." So taking the root meanings: to take what is under, making it straight, and to arise; this instruction can be perfectly applied to sadhana, spiritual practice.

To take the lower impulses of the ego-mind, making it straight through God-remembrance, so that consciousness can rise into spiritual union with our Heavenly Father. Rather than focusing on the body alone as resurrected, this way of understanding the word entails the transformation of the whole inner person,

Jesus, the son of man, becomes Jesus Anointed—the Son of God. And in his wake, we, those he commanded, are to follow in his footsteps. For the Master said, "And he who does not take his cross and followeth me is not worthy of me" (Matthew 10:38).

———

As our dear Lahiri Mahasia Baba prescribed—striving, striving, striving, behold, one day the Goal! There is a saying that, "Rust never sleeps," so too, with ignorance; it never goes on vacation. Every day proves the necessity for striving in our spiritual practice. Ego's default is to seek out the muddy puddles of ignorance—where it feels at home. However, there comes a day, through ever-deepening practice, when we feel more at home swimming in the Ocean of Light and Bliss, inwardly attuned to Spirit—this, then, is the *new normal*.

—⁂—

One may ask, "How do I discriminate between true spiritual masters who made missteps on the way up and those who portray themselves as spiritual adepts, but in reality, they are hypocrites, wolves in sheep's clothing?" For that, we carefully observe—what happens next?

When one falls, then tries to cover it up, continues to stumble from one fall, to another, and casts the blame on others while not doing the hard work to change oneself—that is the very definition of a hypocrite. When, on the other hand, following a fall, the aspirant continues to strive for God; through repentance, or turning away from temptation, the sincere seeker makes reparations where possible, and through intense sadhana, deepens meditation, humility, and surrender thereby coming into contact with the fabric of God's Being, and is renewed in Spirit—then that one grows, and in time he or she is perfected.

A humble tenacity that never gives up, and never gives in, is a sign of a true, aspiring spiritual master.

—⁂—

The sign of a champion athlete is not that he or she never stumbles, but that he or she never gives up. So, too, for the spiritual champion. One may take a knock, but what comes next is not to grovel in the mud and give up, but to pick oneself up, wash the muck off, heal the wounds, and get right back on the path to Self-realization.

⁓⁓

What is "below" the surface is experienced, if we are fortunate, in glimpses of a greater Reality—something we know exists but are not very conscious of, even with the glimpses. To get to this greater Reality, we must face a thin film of reality known as the subconscious mind—through dreams and introspection, we gain a greater awareness of the subconscious mind—those thoughts and emotions that are stored from times past.

Sometimes these memories are compressed psychic energy, compressed because they have been repressed. This reservoir of psychic energy can be a powerful player in a life, making fears and desires create useful and destructive habits that come to us from surprising depths.

This psychic energy holds our past; that is, the good, the bad, and the ugly, all ready to bubble up to the surface, potentially costing us an enormous amount of mental energy; especially wish to keep at bay.

⁓⁓

In my sadhana, God systematically withdrew from me so many personal landmarks: first, the mahasamadhi of my guru, then the loss of a first marriage, family, home, and profession, taking me through two years of a "Dark Night of the Soul." My sadhana stripped me to the bone, then ground the bones to dust, and blew the dust to the four corners of the earth.

I took a sabbatical from being a minister, stating, "I am empty. How could I serve others when I had nothing, not a thing, I can give?"

~⊗~

Life can challenge us to the core, and if the goal is high (And what is higher than God-realization?), then the price must be steep. To paraphrase Krishna in the Gita: fight the good fight with all your strength and be ever focused on God. Whether you win or lose in the outer sense is not in your control, that is up to Me (God). But whether you win or lose, by staying focused on Me, you win the spiritual battle by being aligned with truth and ever advancing in Self-realization.

~⊗~

Learn to identify that sweet spot where you hold up the highest and most transforming ideals, then be skillful in life—be right on the learning edge that yields the greatest benefit to you, and those around you. Sure, you must demand more from yourself, strive to be more; this is absolutely necessary to make progress. But keep it positive, close to home, take joy when you note progress, and when you fall short of your lofty goals, take notes to learn from your experience.

Learn with love and joy in your heart, and in doing so, you will draw invisible forces to aid you in fulfilling the tasks you have assigned for yourself in this life. You cannot make yourself perfect through self-will, but through valiant and persistent spiritual effort, you can touch the fabric of God's Being, and in touching Perfection, you are perfected.

—∞—

In the life of a sadhaka, there can come plateaus—times when it seems there is no progress. This is a sign that you have run up against an inner obstacle of some sort. Not all obstacles come in the form of freight trains that run you over; many come in dark whispers, or stuck energy; these signs are a call to action.

—∞—

Happy is the person who is in harmony with his or her soul's purpose.

—∞—

We thrive best when, like a farmer or gardener, we feel in sync with the seasons; in sync with the time to prepare new ground and sow seeds, and to water and fertilize those seeds and watch them sprout and grow toward the light, to gather the fruit of those labors in a grateful harvest, and then, finally, to enter a winter-time rest.

In that time of rest, we focus on the still-state from which all creation comes. And, when God is ready, new cycles of growth begin anew. Of course, life does not always operate in such defined beginnings, middles, and ends as a farmer's life does, but if we pay attention, we will see such cycles operating in our lives.

As happens in any hero's journey worth its salt, the hero may fail to live up to the standards of a noble path along the way. But, the hero does not give up; rather, he or she recovers and keeps going—that is what makes it a hero's journey.

And that is our hero's journey: we recover, and we keep going no matter what.

Sometimes the lurking opposition is not so obvious—a subtle force behind the scenes makes us shy away from going deeper. It is not until we really challenge it that the obstacle reveals its vicious tenacity and its true name. Thus, we can remain only surface-deep in our devotions, pretending everything is all right, but all the time, not making real spiritual progress.

We must work at keeping ourselves on the edge of growth—not overstraining, and not slacking, yet ever looking to improve.

The most important part of this Work we do for God and Gurus has to do with the individual progress of every aspirant.

Knowing your purpose in life is essential to all; lose that purpose and you lose not only your direction in life, but also hope, and the value of life itself.

A solar flare from our distant sun can interfere with a radio broadcast here on Earth, and so does the static of restless thoughts and ceaseless activity make hearing subtle communications between people unheard.

One of the beautiful things about life in the astral worlds is that thought transference occurs naturally without misinterpreted words getting in the way. Even as writing is a poor substitute for a perfect memory, so spoken words is a poor imitation of thought transference.

To properly reboot your body and mind, they must be turned off—we must have a significant shift during meditation.

We can retreat in life or fight for progress. Each day, we are on a battlefield of some sort, and each day, we decide what we are to do.

No matter what role God has you play in your life, may you sally forth in joy and happy anticipation for what the Infinite has in store for you, knowing that even if you may have some dark moments to face, and roaring dragons to slay, you have the greatest Ally possible at your side—at all times and in all places.

From the beginning of my Spiritual Quest that God set me on, my spiritual practice was driven by necessity as well as by a spirit of scientific inquiry.

───※───

It is our inborn Light of Dharma that demands that we awaken to this greater Reality. We close our eyes, go within, and awareness can expand out to the furthest reaches of the space within.

───※───

Searching

Pilgrimage begins long before you set foot out of the door to go on one. It is best for a pilgrimage to originate as a calling, a deep inner prompting that goes beyond a yearning to travel and see new places. That is because a pilgrimage is a journey of the soul that takes on the guise of traveling to holy sites and meeting spiritual personalities.

—————

All experiences should bring you closer to God. So, do not be thrown by the endless variety life displays to you; each experience is a test for you to see the Divine Spirit in every aspect of His creation.

—————

One of the remarkable things about our spiritual path is that the benefit of its practice is not just for an imagined future, but it is realized in the here and now.

—————

Human love of God means you aspire, pray, and love God more than the world. That is, you have an overwhelming need and drive for God-consciousness, truth, bliss, expansive awareness, and Universal Vision that supersedes your greedy, lustful, self-centered way of life.

This striving for higher consciousness uses the power of attraction that is generated by powerful love to purify your mind and lift you into the supreme consciousness of God.

Prayer is a very large and important topic, and oftentimes its real power is little understood.

It was not until I was nineteen years old and in emotional turmoil that I reached out to God due to the pain I was in, "God! I do not know if You exist, but if You do, if I have never needed You before, I need You now!" Immediately, the pain was alleviated, it felt as if thousands of pounds of crushing pressure were lifted from me. This was a turning point in my life, and it sent me on a journey of exploration for Who and What God is, and for that matter; who and what I am.

A crucial decision you make in life is when you make a commitment to be a life-long learner. It is a theme you can, and need to, commit to daily. To learn from your experience is the basis for all personal and spiritual growth.

You must be able to observe yourself and others accurately, then discriminate between what works and does not work for your good, and, for the highest good of all concerned—this is the way to learn from experience.

Even though the saying has been made famous—Space, the final frontier—I think the true ultimate frontier is inner space through spiritual evolution.

—∞∞∞—

Be still, and know God as the eternal Self of your Being, the Source of unending bliss, and the answer to all of your heart's desires.

—∞∞∞—

Knowing our purpose in life is a remarkably important thing to realize, and to fulfill—for purpose is closely tied to life itself.

For some, purpose changes in life, and what had been a clear purpose earlier, now no longer fits. This change can require painful adjustments, all needed in order to keep in sync with the soul's purpose.

To know and follow our true purpose is the greatest adventure, for the soul's ultimate purpose leads us to our spiritual Home—God-realization.

—∞∞∞—

Why have you taken incarnation? While achieving goals is necessary, why are you here?

You may find there are a lot of activities you are doing that have nothing to do with why you are here; in fact, this busyness actually keeps you from accomplishing essential things in your life.

—∞∞∞—

Check in with your deeper Self—is there any unacknowledged purpose you do not yet consciously acknowledge, or you have been pushing into the background?

The first thing to do is to discover your true purpose in life—first things first!

Every life has purpose, even if your body does not cooperate in any other way, your purpose can be to be a prayer warrior for God.

—⁓—

Purpose is not something that can be handed to you, it is something you must discover for yourself.

—⁓—

The sattvic way moves you toward the mark. The body and mind slow down; alert calmness allows you to tune in to your soul's purpose: a purpose that comes from a very deep part of you. When you tap into this deep part, you simply know that your purpose has been true for you from before you were born.

—⁓—

To be alive to your purpose brings life-energy, enthusiasm, and creativity—all life-affirming attributes.

—⁓—

Seek always to serve God and each other by first immersing yourself in Divine communion, then let all activity be guided by that inner Source; in this way, you will help bring about the transformation of this world to become a haven of peace and goodness for all.

—⁓—

The Galilean Master said that there is no greater act than to give your life in service to others, and surely radiating God-consciousness to one and all is a means of fulfilling this sacred duty.

As long as you have consciousness, and as long as you commune with the Lord of this universe, then you may be a blessing to one and all by transmitting powerful vibrations of the Supreme Consciousness of God.

THE WORK

God-remembrance is not simply another task—it is our primary task. Not only that, but just as importantly, staying connected with God—our real Self—brings important benefits that will actually help us in our worldly life. These benefits are the real secret in life so that we can have both a full and a fulfilling life.

⸺⸙⸺

As aspirants, we too must take responsibility for making our best effort, to recognize the value and synergy from being on a team of devotees: "For where two or three are gathered in my name, there I am in the midst of them" (Matthew 18:20).

The guru-coach helps us to make superlative individual and collective effort, and is ever directing us toward being victorious—that we might all become one with God and help lift this world into higher consciousness.

⸺⸙⸺

It takes time and practice to clear the body system of the attraction of the five senses and to immerse the little self into God alone.

However, living in the freedom and bliss of God makes whatever little effort expended in sadhana seem insignificant in what is given in return.

To make true spiritual progress, the world needs to be set aside. In the pursuit of a calm equanimity, the twin stimulants of tamasic and rajasic (depressive and activating) qualities are known to be the impediments to attaining conscious union with the Divine.

One must surmount the qualities of this age to go beyond the things of the body, to ascend to things of the Spirit.

—❧—

It is important that your needs and your possessions are in the right proportion to your life. Master used to say, "Simple living and high thinking." Simple living and high thinking mean that your possessions are right sized to your needs, and your thoughts are upon God and upon being of service to this world. When you have mastered this balance, you will feel harmony with your surroundings, and you will know a sense of freedom that no material wealth can ever give you.

—❧—

Let simple living and high thinking be our mantra for finding the golden middle path. Like the musician who, unknowingly, was the teacher of the Buddha when he told his student, "Do not over-tighten the stringed instrument or it will break, and do not allow it to be too loose or it will not make the proper sound."

Continuously work to find the right balance in your life and then feel the freedom promised through the golden middle path of simple living and high thinking.

—❧—

It can seem crazy for anyone to choose unhappiness, and yet we know from first-hand experience that we do exactly that. The natural question comes, "Why?" The answers can vary, but it comes down to the same thing—a part of us thinks a negative thought will make us safe and happy. For instance, a state of depression can seem like a safe place to retreat. A child may seek out a closet, make a nest of blankets and pillows inside and close the closet door to darken the room. Inside the closet all the chaos, shame, and fear disappear. Depression can initially feel like that closet, all safe and warm.

And every other "negative" behavior has a root cause in seeking happiness—but in all the wrong places. Again, "Why?" Because we are not one whole person yet. We have many parts to ourselves, parts that vie with one another for fulfillment of varied needs. The key to resolving this inner conflict can be found in learning some basic spiritual principles, and then teaching them to all the various parts of ourselves.

───

When I have faith and confidence in my own judgements, then what others think will not be *swallowed whole*, rather I will listen openly to what another thinks, and measure it by what I know to be true.

I use my reason and my intuition to sense the truth.

───

Because the brain is not used to seeing the value in knowing God, it overlooks what it already knows; much like seeing, but not seeing, the chair in the room. Spiritual practice is learning the necessity to know God.

Until the brain fully appreciates the value of Bliss, Light, and intuitional Wisdom that can only come from the Divine Presence, it will treat the whole idea like a foreign concept that it chooses not to see or feel.

———

Humankind is capable of the highest consciousness; however, as we see signs daily, it often times responds to its lowest nature. When we, as humans, put our minds upon attaining supreme God-consciousness, then the battle between lowest and highest natures ensues. Lowest nature is selfish, greedy, fearful, and it can be vicious. Highest nature is loving, kind, and full of service.

———

As I witnessed firsthand, with both Mother Hamilton and Swami Satchidananda, a spiritual life is not hiding from the difficult parts of life and all of its complexities; rather, it is often putting yourself right into the middle of it.

The difference is that you have now placed yourself on God's side; there is no separation, *and that makes all the difference.*

———

As we evolve as a race of humankind, it is ennobling to think of raising this planet's consciousness into the highest realms of Spirit; a heaven in, and on, earth.

———

Master said, "Be a smile millionaire," Papa said, "See God in everyone you meet," Mother Hamilton said, "Keep your mind on God," Mother Teresa said, "Do something beautiful for God," Swami Satchidananda said, "Expand your circle of love daily," Jesus said, "What you have done to the least of these my bretheren, ye have done it unto me" (Matthew 25:40). These great ones in God remind us that every day we can directly do something to improve this world.

———❦———

I alone am responsible for seeing or not seeing higher reality; I cannot expect the world to see it first.

———❦———

Exercise self-mastery—focus on your own higher nature.

Continue in your own Light and remain undisturbed by what another says or does.

This does not make you a doormat; you may even tell them *to get the hell out!* But you do not lose connection to that vast aspect of yourself that is beneath the surface—your greater qualities.

———❦———

Be determined to be master of yourself, and as a result experience freedom, bliss, and a universal vision. You need not torture your body in order to do this, even as the Buddha taught the Middle Way—avoiding extremes. You will find that focusing on starving the body or trying to make the mind empty without the uptake of blissful joy and spiritual freedom will not free you.

—◦◦◦—

We encounter disappointment, loss, and jolts to our system on a fairly regular basis on this material plane; they are, and will always be, part of our lives here. To weather these storms when they hit us and not allow them to knock us off balance must be a deep part of our spiritual practice.

—◦◦◦—

Decision making goes right to the heart of how we live our lives. From deciding what to eat to whether we buy a new car, or house, or make a business or professional decision—decisions are an important part of everyone's life.

—◦◦◦—

With mindfully caring for the things you have been given, you work to bind yourself to God-consciousness, making that your primary relationship in life. In doing so, you can expect to have freedom from anxiousness—to feel peace in the midst of activity; you will intuitively know that the decisions you make are for the higher good of all, and you will fulfill the purpose for which you have taken incarnation.

—◦◦◦—

The mind directs our life-energy, emotions, and moods; change the mind and all else will follow.

With your mind, wherever it goes, the rest of you will follow. Change your thoughts, change your life.

———⟨∞⟩———

By meditating regularly and deeply, you change not only your life, but your family's life, your community, and even the world at large. There is simply no way for you to accurately assess all the ways that your spiritual practice is absolutely needed by this world.

Therefore, resolve that whatever role you are playing in this world, you play it well, and you enter into your spiritual practice with all of your heart, mind, and soul—for you are God's emissary.

———⟨∞⟩———

There is a saying, when you are faced with a decision: do what is more difficult; it is usually the right choice.

———⟨∞⟩———

As followers of this path, we have been given the highest, most powerful principles and techniques for spiritual evolution, for ourselves as well as for the world at large. It is up to each one of us to fulfill the vision that Jesus, Babaji, and all the masters have for us.

We may not be able to force the world to be how we would like it, but we can change ourselves, and therefore be agents of change for others.

———⟨∞⟩———

Then there is Swami Ramdas' creed of universal love and service. Putting into place this maxim brings hearts and minds together in marching toward the fulfillment of what humankind is really intended to be. Universal love and service is not a difficult idea to understand, only its practice requires self-mastery—your little self that leads you to anger, greed, and fear needs to be replaced with pure perception—seeing that the world is God.[3]

—•—

We have been given the very best tools to gain the highest consciousness: Kriya yoga meditation, chanting, keeping our mind on God, serving Him in all we do and in whom all we meet, and divinely loving Him is all-inclusive and propels us to ultimate fulfillment as a modern householder yogi.

—•—

God creates us, He sustains us, and when it is His will, He withdraws us back into His Being. He is our well-wisher, yet there may be certain things we have to go through. It may be the result of our own doing in the moment, something from a distant, unremembered past, or from the collective karma of the world we live in.

—•—

Even when dealing with unknowable origins, we can yet say, "A true understanding is that spirituality is a science." We begin with a spiritual practice, and when the

---

3   www.anandashram.org

experiment is carried out exactly as prescribed, the results are predictable.

Perform Kriya Yoga and the spine will be spiritually charged: the light of God is seen, the sound of God is heard, the mind is purified and consciousness expands and becomes Self-realized, or: chant God's name, think on His attributes, surrender yourself at His feet, and your mind will be purified; you will live in bliss; consciousness will rise above the mundane, and you will know God— merge with Him.

Your heart, mind, and soul are the experimental labs in which these procedures are carried out, the outcome, as predicted, is the transformation of consciousness from the human to the Divine.

⸺⸰⸎⸰⸺

There is a big difference between reading and agreeing with wisdom from great spiritual masters and actualizing it in our interior lives. Constant practice is required.

Repeated times of *standing up with a bright face and a brighter heart*, impress upon the brain that it really does lift us above the problems faced in this worldly existence.

⸺⸰⸎⸰⸺

The scriptures take on a completely new meaning when you see that they apply to you in a most specific way. To think that Jesus, or any emissary from God, is the only one to go through such experiences and you are to be simply drawn along on someone's coattails, without anything for you to do but have faith, is a very pale view of a spiritual life.

On the other hand, to know that Jesus came to show the Way, with the intention that you are to follow every step, makes the scriptures become vital—essential to you and your life.

—∞∞—

We must choose, we must allow Him to open those stubborn doors, to love the world through us, and few can let the love of God shine through their actions toward all.

It is only then when the love of God shines that we will have unbounded love passing through us, we may then bathe in a vast ocean of peaceful love, making us complete—for the first time, we are truly whole.

—∞∞—

Jesus fell three times while carrying his cross—or the body—up the hill of Golgotha—meaning Hill of the Skull (i.e., ascending spinal consciousness to the higher centers of the brain). Of course, this story of Christ from two thousand years ago is conveying what happens in everyone's spiritual journey to complete realization.

When we are put through the Mystical Crucifixion, we are tempted, and tempted hard, even as Peter was in his fearful denial of Jesus. In that temptation, we may fall—three times, the Christ fell, and he was born an incarnation of Divinity.

—∞∞—

The path of the cross, is the path to resurrection—from pain of separation to the bliss, light, and wisdom of the

Perfect One. This is the true assurance that you have so long been looking for—knowing that God is with you always.

⸺◦◦◦⸺

Right action, or dharma, is the most efficient means forward, both in this world and spiritually. While wrong action can look more expedient in the moment, it inevitably builds resistant karma that immediately, or eventually, causes you suffering, and undermines your success.

⸺◦◦◦⸺

To think of Master Paramhansa Yogananda with total devotion will draw him near, and will make you know that his grace and blessings are flowing to you; they will change you and draw you closer to God in body, mind, and soul.

Master came to make you know that you may realize God—it is for this reason only that he was born. You can honor him most by going to work, and even as he did, make Self-realization your priority—first, middle, and last.

⸺◦◦◦⸺

Sri Yukteswarji gave us a metric for knowing God, Do you experience ever-new joy? Swami Satchidananda gave us another: Is your circle of love growing larger every day? For Mother: Do you continuously keep your mind dwelling on God? Master asks: Do you dive deeper in your daily meditations until you get God contact? Lahiri Mahasaya: Do you perceive your true Self at the ajna? Babaji states: It is your humble service to humankind that the Lord finds pleasing above all. And Papa's ideal: Continuously chant Ram Nam.

Here are measurements, metrics for your spiritual path. Read each of these again; make them a challenge; let your practice dive deeper and soar higher—answer the call of your Soul to know God, and be a blessing to this world.

———

We honor the guru and the guru-lineage for what we have been given. We make certain we are not "the poor work-man blaming his tools," but that we are ready to go to work and fully engaged with the truth and the guru-shakti that the powerful guru gives.

We strive to take the Light that has been freely given, and in return, we give the Light we now know within to all the world, sharing that Light in all that we do. For, to really honor the guru means that we do what he or she asks us to do, to give as he or she gives, to emulate the guru in all the important ways–to be an emissary of truth. There is no greater way to honor the guru.

———

Marriage cannot be a simple "Happily ever after," but that does not mean it cannot be the most meaningful and loving relationship you can have on a human basis. It is the working out of life that can either draw you closer together to solve the many problems faced or it can tear you apart. To be connected to God within, letting Him guide you, awaken love in you, and give you the cour-age to open yourself fully in the presence of another, is the greatest ally you have in bringing out the best in a marriage.

In the end, marriage is your practice ground for your oneness with the Infinite Beloved, and being one with Him in all of what life brings to your doorstep, "For better, for worse, to love and to cherish, in sickness and in health, in prosperity and in adversity." Amen!

This world is on an evolutionary climb out of the Dark Ages, and, yes, there are challenges; however, with God in our heart, this is a new day, a bright day full of promise and glory. God is on the move, and whether the world around us reflects that or not, it is certainly true for us as we lead the way into the path of joy, light, and abundance—Grace operating within, without, and all about.

Let us put our mind on God, put our mind on God, put our mind on God, and our life is changing already—feel the peace and joy of His ever-abiding Presence right in our heart and soul. Learn what it is to live a life without fear, always aware of His ever-abiding Grace residing in our heart, mind, and soul. Be it so!

In the face of so much of what we see and hear of selfish disregard for others, what are we to think? What are we to do? The most basic teaching is one that can be understood by all; it is called the Golden Rule: Do to others what you would have done to you—in other words, treat others exactly the way you want to be treated. There it is, a little thoughtfulness about what that means to each of us would make this world a heaven on earth. To start the ball rolling, let us start by embodying this principle in our own life from this day out—be kind, considerate, truthful, and compassionate.

—∞∞—

Karma Yoga is the foundation for spiritual living. Karma means action: it is what you physically do in life. You are to live a life of purity, starting with eating healthy foods in moderation—not with avarice; you work, and do all in the spirit of service to God in others—not for greed; and all that you speak, is in concert with the highest truth you know—do not lie. In your spiritual quest, you build the foundation of your spiritual life with actions that match what you know to be in the highest light.

—∞∞—

We come into this life with missions to accomplish. We need only look at those recurring themes in our life for hints as to what we have come to do: for some, it is education and learning, having and raising a family, a profession and trade, a passion for a sport, hobby, or craft, and having a loyal group of friends—all can be a big part of our lives. Some of these can seem rather pedestrian; others are vital. However, what is important to one may hold absolutely no meaning for another—the fact you hold it as valuable is what makes it important.

—∞∞—

All creation begins with an idea on a causal level: everything starts with a conception. Not all ideas achieve physical manifestation—some fulfill themselves as an idea only. And some concepts are seeds for the future—they will not see manifestation immediately but continue to hold great power for their eventual result.

—◦◦◦—

If you do not need to know God to start this journey, then what does it mean to put your mind on God? It means you focus your mind in a singular fashion, in the highest way you know. You may repeat the name of God without any great knowledge of what God is in the beginning, practice the mantra Hong Sau without knowing the great I AM—in fact, truthfully, you will not fully know God, or who your real Self is, until you have become realized.

—◦◦◦—

When you have rule of law, but there is no love and compassion, then true justice will ultimately be sacrificed. When you have government and ruling bodies, and there is no love as a guiding light, they will become corrupt, and government will not produce the greatest general good. When you have businesses, and there is no love behind its intention or its practice, then its goods and services will not truly benefit society.

◦◦◦

Every human misery can trace its roots back to wrong motive, which results in wrong action.

My purpose was not more important than my friend who was to become a welder, my father who grew a business, or anyone else who was in step with their true purpose in life. What is important, even essential, is that each person is in step with his or her own purpose and that this purpose is life affirming and growth producing.

Let us practice, practice, practice until we are living in the "spiritual zone" and feeling God's joyful Presence within us, until we are centered in our deeper Self, no matter our outer circumstances, and our inborn dharma spontaneously guides us to right action.

By enacting the "spiritual zone" practice we receive life-giving energy (supplying us with far more than we give in our practice). It is not simply another task to add to our "to do list," it the one indispensable thing to do when fulfilling daily duties in this world while serving our Infinite Beloved.

In addition to the normal functions in humankind, and nature, prana (life-energy) plays an active role in the next evolutionary step of transforming the human into the Divine.

As soon as you are aware of being stalled, you must make a sincere and intense effort to put your mind back on God.

You sense the stall, and a lack of progress, when feeling inwardly neutral, or there is a growing desire-nature for this world that outdistances your desire for God. When you are aware of these counter feelings, you fiercely cut away all oppositional thoughts and desires the moment they show up, avoid temptations, chant God's name, and meditate until God-contact is made—these are the ways you can power through a stall.

Begin your day in meditation, focus on God until you make contact, then enter into your day feeling that peace and joy in activities. At the end of the day: meditate on God, withdrawing all the day's activities back into God-consciousness. In this way you replicate in a micro-sense what God does in the macrocosm.

Our inner spiritual life goes in cycles. So, do not become dulled to new life surging forward in spiritual practice. Be sure to put in the hard work to increase those sacred seeds in their growth; reap the harvest of peace, bliss, and joy. Then let us merge our little self with the Supreme Self in complete stillness.

Our spiritual life reflects, like all of life, these cycles—let us stay alive to our own rhythm of growth so that we may reap God's great harvest.

Giving thanks is an affirmation for what is even now coming to you in multifarious ways.

———∞———

Meditation, exercise, saving money, not watching too much television (Master called it a pest in the home in the early 1950s), and breaking addictions can be difficult in the moment. However, its after-effect is that you feel better, healthier, and more joyful. So, it is really about taking a moment to sense the total package concerning a certain activity. Ask: Does this bring me joy?

———∞———

Since it is an inevitability that we one day discover God within and without, then joy-filled bliss must be in our future. That being the case, and God being all goodness in life, then it only makes sense to accelerate our growth in God as fast as possible!

———∞———

Purpose uplifts any activity you are engaged in when it is aligned with why you are here. For instance, if being in service to God is your purpose, then going to a work in which you see yourself serving God in your customer or the useful role that your product plays in people's lives, elevates any beneficial work that is dharmic into seva—loving service to others. All activities, sweeping the floor, washing dishes, driving somewhere, educating yourself—any and all activities in alignment with purpose make the activity worthy and fulfilling.

What is essential is that you know why you have come—that as long as you are drawing breath there is yet purpose for you to fulfill.

Purpose is inspiring, life-giving, and in accomplishing it you truly know that you will feel profound satisfaction. There will not be a thousand of such purposes in your life; there will be a comparatively few. Your purpose may be to connect with a profession, family, and children, some service to do in life, the perfection of some art or creative endeavor, or purpose can relate to physical achievements such as a sport or perfect health. Purpose can relate to any topic at all, but it must rise to the standard of being connected with the real reason you were born.

Some choose to defer decisions to others and not get involved, but actively informed citizen-yogis help keep things on track. One does not need to watch every thrust and blow in hand-to-hand political combat, but to stay abreast of the evolving issues and tuning in to how God directs you on each issue is consistent with being a responsible citizen with the privilege to vote. This makes for a better, albeit imperfect, system.

Now, it is up to me to utilize each day for His glory and to manifest His Light through all that I think, do, and say.

There are two great joys in my life right now. The first is to see aspirants with both feet on the path: striving, working, loving and giving heart, mind, and soul to the Divine Quest. And not just that, but showing signs of progress: skin shining, eyes glittering, bliss, and love filling their cups to overflowing. It is not that every day we must look like a front-page cover for Enlightenment Today, not when there are dark nights to be endured and heavy burdens that must be carried. But a general trend up.

What started as a spark, became a flame, and now, our aim is to become a blazing sun of aspiration.

A realignment of the body, mind, and Spirit can reboot our system, making for maximal function. One of the simplest ways for doing this is in our bi-daily meditation. We may begin our meditation with our thinking-software wasting mental computing power by looping certain thoughts, and our body-hardware tense and out of sorts. Now, if we spend our entire meditation time simply stuck in these loops, or thinking about what is going wrong in our body or our life, that is not meditation at all, and it will definitely not reboot our system.

Go within and realize that the great Reality is waiting to resurrect itself within. Words do not do it; reading will not get us there.

Only by knowing that the Kingdom of Heaven is within, will we come face to face with the living Christ.

———⊗⊗⊗———

Yoga is a practical philosophy with measurable goals to be attained in physical health and enlightenment.

———⊗⊗⊗———

The Self always takes action for the highest good of everyone concerned and leads the soul to ultimate spiritual freedom.

———⊗⊗⊗———

I do all that I can to maintain perfect health. While knowing I am not this body, yet it is my part to be its good steward—so that I may continue to serve God and Gurus in all I do.

———⊗⊗⊗———

We are faced with many challenges in life. How we face those challenges determines the quality of our lives. We can be fear factories, or engines for success. Once the fear factory is put into action, it tends to run on its own recycled energy, unless intentionally shut down. Fear generates fear; only calmness brings the fear factory to a standstill.

———⊗⊗⊗———

WHEN THE WORLD INTRUDES

We stand at a crossroads. The world offers much in technology, conveniences, entertainment and distractions; from a spiritual standpoint, all of this is worthless and an obstruction.

—◊◊◊—

This world acts as a maze of a thousand turns that keep us from the hidden Goal. However, these same great knowers of God that tell us about the glowing kingdom within also give us the means for traversing the maze quickly and safely.

—◊◊◊—

It is inevitable that when we mix with the world, we will pick up some lower influences. Advanced practitioners may rise above these influences. Some may be divinely directed to purify such forces through their three bodies (material, astral and causal) and the most advanced in consciousness will simply see these forces as aspects of God.

—◊◊◊—

There are subtle reasons for an inwardly-focused meditator to find a suitable cave. As you spiritually progress your psychic body becomes more sensitive, more open. Noise, light, and mental disturbances by worldly people can become difficult, even painful for the ardent seeker.

The refuge of the cave blocks out sound and light and is an excellent insulator from the psychic chaos of the world.

The key to finding your way through a situation is whether you take your mind off God or you keep your attention upon the One. You may still feel pain, distress, anger, and frustration, but with a perfected consciousness there is not a cloud of separation from the light of God; in fact, your mind goes deeper into God.

Tragedy comes into the home in many ways. Sickness and Death are two common ways, but there are also tragedies of stealing, lying, cruel words, domestic violence, and silent withholding. These are some familiar tragedies that too often snake their way into the home.

You should not be discouraged or doubtful when faced with the oppositional force you see in the world, and sometimes right within your own self. Rather, you should use these painful events as reminders that you are called to a higher life and heed the call of those great God-men and God-women who have gone before you.

I came up against a case of murderous anger in a soul; in reality, this anger stemmed from a deep fear. In self-absorption, this individual felt the world was not meeting certain needs. Such anger and fear is not uncommon, but how sad it is when it results in a looping dialogue for which there is no solution.

It is because fear and anger are emotionally charged and self-sustaining; if there is a change in one area of dissatisfaction in life, then another will crop up that will be found to be equally dissatisfying. Thus, fear and anger lead to a never-ending cycle. This person's anger clung to me like cigarette smoke permeates clothes and hair and everything it touches.

The real solution is to realize the Divine Intention behind all the world's activities, even the bad and the ugly. With this solution alone, a peace that surpasses all understanding comes into the heart and soul—a peace unshakable.

Without this solution, fear and anger will corrupt the soul, making it ugly and distorted behind the recognition of its original design by the Creator.

<hr />

Lower impulses make you feel that your mind is being drawn away from God. You know the limiting, tortured feelings that come from following these desires. Like a honey trap, you are drawn by the cloying sweet sensations inside the trap, but once you enter in, you are encaged. God-experience frees you from the trap, but you must clearly choose God over sweet, deadly promises.

I have known those who were sincere and dedicated upon the path, and then some old habit was re-awakened: drugs, alcohol, sex, and the spark of temptation became a flame—the individual was consumed. Or, the spiritual flame was no longer fed with deepened meditation and intense love of God—the flame died and the spark faded to a bygone memory. The spark that became a flame was now gone, and it seemed but a distant memory.

Temptation can be of any nature, depending upon the psychological makeup of the individual. It can be sex, drugs, fear, greed, power, pride, self-interest to the exclusion to others, lack of surrender, so many aspects to the opposing force—it will always fight against what the inner soul knows to be true and correct.

If your spiritual life does not inform you about the way you make decisions, then it has not penetrated deeply enough into your life. For some, simply making the decision to meditate daily and attending Center meetings may feel enough. But once you enter into your everyday life, there may be little carryover; you suddenly revert to habits that may or may not serve you. It bears examination to observe how your spiritual life moves into the most basic ways you live.

Chronic fear gets us nowhere, and can render us inert or direct us in absolutely the wrong direction.

———∞———

If clouds are building on the horizon, then we should take precautions—this is wise. But there is a line between having a concern and falling into worry. A concern comes with a focus upon taking action to improve a situation, a worry is mentally running a race with no purpose and no end. Worry can become a habit that is mindless and destructive.

———∞———

Worldly cares can sap youthfulness right out of your being. God can just as easily pour Himself in and fill you with light and joy overflowing. Yes, this world alternates between highs and lows–it ever has, and it will ever be so. However, in your oneness with the Infinite, you are His evermore—knowing this is the key to lasting happiness.

———∞———

This is a tremendous life God has given us. Surely, there are times when life tests us hard, straining us to the limit of human endurance. There are other times when things seem to go so smoothly—both can be tests for our loyalty to God. Do we forget Him? Do emotions becloud our judgement and obscure Him?

When life is hard, do we seek out His power, wisdom, and comfort, or feel sorry for ourselves and have a pity party of one? Or if things go wonderfully smoothly, do we bow in wonder and awe at what He has brought about? Or do we feel we can do without God: ego thinks, "I am the clever one; I am riding high and do not need attunement with anything, or anyone, much less with God?"

———

Naturally, from a human standpoint, we like to have things go easy. For some, when a transition takes something away and makes life more challenging, we can feel betrayed. Somewhere inside, we feel that if we are making spiritual effort, then everything should go perfectly smoothly in this world.

However, we do live in world of duality, and the alternating currents will always be at work, bringing both, from a human standpoint, good and bad situations. While it is true that leading a spiritual life will avoid many a painful trap in life, no one can avoid all difficulties, and at times, hardships seem to come bundled up and delivered all at once.

———

Those committing terrible acts must be stopped and stopping them is a loving act for the villain as well as the victim, because although the victimizer may be jailed and face consequences for these actions, the villain is prohibited from further heinous actions which would continue to further darken his or her soul.

———

As spiritual aspirants, the crux of living in this world is for us to fully participate in it, and not to be separated from our true Self as a result. Events can come rapid fire; for example, demands to make decisions, to make the body and mind function even when they are resistant to doing so. Each success brings its own challenges, tempting you to think that you are the doer.

———

If we want justice, then we must treat others justly; if we want respect, then we must begin by giving it. With every word and action, we create, then we reap what we have set into motion.

———

This life is a voyage of God-discovery, and our family is not a distraction, but the very means by which we attain the universal vision.

———

You need not despair that you live in organized-chaos; rather, you need only find the balance in life that anchors you in the Divine; thereby, live your life while maintaining a higher meaning and an inner source of joy that is not dependent on there being smooth waters around you.

———

Sometimes a computer problem can be solved with a quick restart. In meditation terms, we take a few minutes during the day to reset our body-mind-Spirit system.

Other times, the computer needs a whole system shut down, we then wait for some time for a cold-restart—meditation-wise, this means going deeper and soaring higher until we have the solution and freedom we are looking for.

—⊶⊷—

Truth means we do not distort the reality—truth goes to the heart of the matter with clarity; truth should not be swayed with emotion or bias.

—⊶⊷—

Better to lead a life of balance, fulfill your duties in life, and purify your body and mind by being "in the world, not of the world."

—⊶⊷—

The mind is very quick and will slip into the familiar worry pathway unless governed and taught to choose a more positive mode.

—⊶⊷—

One of the enduring challenges for aspirants comes with relationships we have in this world, through family, friends, and professions. The fine line of how *to be in this world but not of it,* offers a demanding obstacle course to run, but like all obstacle courses, they are intended to make us better, stronger.

—⊶⊷—

Yogacharya David, Haridwar, India, 2005.

Love and Truth

DEEPER

There are some areas where seeing how much there is to know can be disheartening, but not with God. With spiritual realization, there is only awe and inspiration to know that when we reach for the infinite, there is a promise of more Light, more bliss, and more revelations of deeper Truth! It is inspiring beyond all words.

―⁂―

"Come, follow me," (Matthew 4:19). Jesus said this to his direct disciples, and he says this to all of us. To follow him means to live as he lived, to know what he knew, to be even as he was: a Son of God. "Follow me," not in blind belief, but see with your own eyes, hear with your own ears, know with your own mind, the same as he saw, heard, and knew—his heavenly Father. He calls to us even now, "Come, follow me."

―⁂―

The obstacles and challenges in our life are not mere irritants, but God testing us to look to Him first, then heroically strive to overcome them. We no longer feel isolated and alone, rather we have a river of love flowing through us to all that we meet; and we feel complete.

―⁂―

One thing about love, it constantly wants to express itself. As I have often said, love is both a noun and a verb. First, it is like the sea, a state of Being content within its expansive Self. And second, love is like a flowing river, always moving and expressing itself. In realizing God, we simultaneously and easily have both aspects of love.

⸻

Realizing Truth will alone free the soul from the thralldom of maya, universal ignorance. This world is rough play. However, when souls love one another, serve one another, and seek the Light within and in one another, this world consciousness is lifted higher, changed for the better, and holds the promise of transforming this world into a peaceful garden, where the lion will lie down with the lamb.

⸻

Build a habit of giving goodness, and it will surely return to you, just as surely as the sun rises in the morning. But, most of all, in marriage you give the best of who you are because it brings out the best in you; it is how God-consciousness is made manifest in this world and it is what brings you true and lasting happiness.

⸻

Belief is something of the mind, but faith comes from some place more fundamental to our being.

Faith is not simply desire or belief; it is true contact with God.

Faith connects the mind, in a viable way, to the supreme power of the Creator and in that connection, the higher power of Grace flows.

—⁓—

Start by feeling peace and upliftment, make God contact during your practice. Then, you can consciously radiate that experience out to your home, community, the world, and creation itself. In feeling the vibrancy in the room, your room then becomes transparent and the power you feel goes out and out as your consciousness expands with this feeling. God Himself is working through you to bless this world.

There is nothing greater in this world than to be a conscious instrument in the hands of the Divine. You and all those sincere in their spiritual practice invisibly unite to lift this world up for much needed harmony, peace, light, and love. In this way, your Temple-home becomes a blessing for one and for all.

—⁓—

I deeply pray that as we begin anew, as in truth we do each and every moment of every day, we establish ourselves in an unshakable freedom, a freedom that is with us no matter our circumstance in life: true spiritual freedom, now and always.

—⁓—

"Oh my Lord, I pray for this world. You are all-powerful, You are everywhere present, awaken Yourself in all humanity. You are the Great Awakener, You are the eternal Light, You are the great Awakener, awaken Yourself in all humanity." And so, on went my prayer out of the depths of my soul.

—∞—

Experience teaches that only when the mind is still is God revealed—this makes all the difference.

—∞—

My heart is wide open as love flows like a vast river. There is no beginning or end, only radiant love shines and moves through to one and all.

It has no demand, nor does it need reciprocity; however, it glows brightly when there is receptivity in another.

It is strong in the physical presence of someone or a group, but it is equally powerful from a distance as well. When I think of another who is far away, there is a distinct awareness that love is transmitted directly to the recipient.

—∞—

I know of no other practice that works so directly with the spine and the brain for the evolution of all three bodies: the physical, astral and causal. The deeper we go in our practice, the more profound are the changes that occur in the subtle spine through breath, focus of mind, and transformative life-energy. We are truly blessed by the intelligent design that has gone into this Kriya practice; it provides for perfect balance.

—∞—

On a human level, we definitely experience being on the battleground between good and evil. Each day is a test of our attraction and love for God, versus our mind's tendency for being seduced into a world of separation from the One. And here is a great secret, once you trace the power for separation back to God, really trace it (not just a half-hearted weak thought), we break the power of separateness—all that which is negative in every thought, word, or action. Darkness hates the light, and cannot co-exist with it.

Once we bring the light of God into the picture as the one true source of all, darkness must depart.

Discover the blissful joy of Christ Consciousness embodied in the life and teachings of Jesus and sleeping in the potential within every human being. Be blessed—dive deep and soar high!

Whether with words or in Wordless Prayer, go deeper into being a conduit for God's will to quicken creation with His power, bliss, love, light, joy, and wisdom. Be a blessing to this world, for every thought you have has creative power.

You must be aware as to whether your thoughts and words are healing and uplifting, or damning and giving power to what is negative (as in gossip). Wordless Prayer is a powerful way of being God's instrument and for you to be a blessing to this world.

One of the great challenges is to refresh our mental screens to see family with fresh eyes, not based on the past, but see God evolve Himself through all forms. Then, we may enjoy God in all His various aspects, and find fresh wonders peeking through old, familiar relationships. This gives new meaning to each one we meet, rather than tired-out scripts from outdated family ties.

—∞∞∞—

Let us practice seeing the best in one and all, seeing the purity of being that each one intrinsically has from his or her Creator. If an individual actively shows progress, then he or she may be given gradual access to new situations to further demonstrate improvements. If old behaviors arise, then distance may be the best feedback for learning, and at the very least, keeping them from further damaging themselves, or others.

Higher spiritual perception does not make one a weak doormat, willing to accept the unacceptable; nevertheless, the devotee always looks to see the higher nature deeply residing in the heart and soul of every soul from God—and where else can a soul come from but from God?

—∞∞∞—

Real happiness consists of aligning thought and action with one's innermost being. Proper alignment equals joy; misalignment produces suffering.

—∞∞∞—

Divine Love is unlike human love that is limited and often-times exists in a quid pro quo—*if you love me well, then I will love you*. Nor is Prem, pure love, sentimental, which can also vacillate—running hot and cold. True Divine Love flows through the heart and is no respecter of whether someone deserves that love; it simply flows.

The urge for freedom of thought and action, the rule of law, a check and balance among governmental entities to prevent abuse; the affirmation that fundamental rights are derived from God and not the caprice of a king, despot, or even an elected government, that citizens elect their leaders and may depose them if they misbehave or abuse their power; that there are certain fundamentals that may not be tampered with, combined with a flexibility for change in law—these were revolutionary ideas of the time—never been tried before—many, most, around the world thought it would fail—and it is a revolution of basic rights and protections that a large portion of humanity still do not have today.

Real love endures and is based on respect and friendship—it is a feeling that resembles the patina of wood. Patina is created through years of usage, and even those things that can be not good for the finish, sunlight, dust, and scuffs, all add to the patina that give it a rich glow that cannot be created in any other way except through time and usage. There are times when love has to endure much, but in the end, it creates a deepening glow that shines all the more with kindness, care, and usage.

———∞———

When we have a ready and simple faith, we find the truth is not far away. Having the willingness to open our heart and mind to the radiant Presence already existing within, reveals the doorway to this most wonder-filled and exciting experience that can be had by all. We do not need to build complicated creeds and beliefs; in fact, that is contrary to the prime simplicity that gets us entry.

Let go of all thoughts that happiness lies out there somewhere and let us open our mind and heart to the divine revelation that is seeking out an opportunity for awakening us now. Let us join together; if not in person, then in spirit, and seek out this omniscient Presence that is also seeking us.

———∞———

To know the truth in its totality, you must have a calm mind. By meditating deeply, you pierce the veil of separation and realize the all-pervasive Spirit—you know truth as God knows it, and through the universal vision, you realize that you cannot be separate from any part of creation.

To perceive truth on this level entails more than always speaking the truth—however, speaking the truth is a pre-requisite to attaining and becoming established in this higher plane of consciousness. Those who lie and try to cover things up and then go on to say they represent the highest truth cannot be what they say they are.

———∞———

The great Master, Jesus, said that when you know the truth, it sets you free—no truer words have ever been spoken.

When truth and love go together, it does not diminish the clarity of truth. There are some very hard realities about life, and people commit acts of evil that should not be swept under the rug. However, as a member of this world, and that world includes the evil which is done, if our outrage for wrong action disconnects us from God and the universal vision, then our emotional reaction cannot be said to represent the whole truth.

———∞———

There is truth with a small "t"—what the truth of a particular situation is—then there is Truth with a capital "T", a direct revelation from the superconscious mind. To really be a life-long learner means that you seek out both levels of truth and Truth: this is the greatest quest in life.

There are many scientists, philosophers, and people of all walks of life who interest themselves in what the truth of a particular situation is; but there are few who take the journey all the way to the Truth of what God is.

———∞———

Truth and truth often come in prime simplicity, going directly to the heart of the matter. Be an explorer of truth and Truth—be forever a life-long learner.

—∞∞—

Bhakti, intense love, and attraction for attaining the supreme state of God-realization, makes the dome for your temple of spiritual practice—that which caps the spiritual life with success. The drawing power of love is required for the kind of complete self-surrender that is necessary to be subsumed in Divine Consciousness.

—∞∞—

Building your spiritual temple by constructing a solid foundation, intelligently designed frames for the upper structure, and a brilliantly radiating dome in your daily life is a wonderful thing; it shows you what is needed in order to realize God. But knowing the way and being immersed in the supreme Reality is not the same thing.

Be inspired by these beautiful teachings: take the complete plunge into spiritual life with total enthusiasm—be absorbed into the Infinite Beloved who dwells beyond time and space and all form—realize the Truth even as the Buddha, Papa Ramdas, and Mother so fully immersed themselves in the highest Reality, and then help others to build their own temples of spiritual practice with nothing but the very finest materials.

—∞∞—

This is a perfect moment, and what the Lord chooses or not chooses is held in His almighty hand.

———&———

There has never been a time when ultimate truth did not exist, only that it became lost to the majority.

———&———

Even though yearning for God can be tremendously painful as your heart breaks in its desire for the universal vision, your increasing devotion now becomes a more powerful force in the psyche and supersedes attachment to the senses.

Bliss, upliftment, joy, loving service, and a positive desire for the Divine fill you and propel you, to the ultimate Goal of goals.

Love and discrimination work together, along with selfless service to others and a growing drive to enter into the highest states of meditative-union that becomes all-consuming.

———&———

Attunement with dharma (right action) leads to spiritual freedom; ignoring or going against those principles of ultimate truths leads to wrong actions, and farther binds the soul in ignorance and darkness.

For dharma to be fulfilled, truth must be combined with compassion, love, and ahimsa (do no harm).

———&———

And Jesus has spoken nothing but the truth, even when it cost him everything. He taught in small groups, he spoke to multitudes, and he never wavered—even when threatened with torture and death. Because Jesus has always spoken the truth, those who are sincere recognize the power of what he says, even when they do not always understand his true meaning. Those closest to him are not immune to his sharp corrections, the keen sword of wisdom that slices ego to the bone—unrelenting, ever vigilant, finely tuned to the verities of his Heavenly Father. We too should follow his example and speak loving truth without compromise.

Attaining the supreme truth reveals that real discernment is always saturated with compassion for all those who strive.

To have a realistic view of the spiritual path upon which we tread, we must know that: "Yes, we can fall," and, "Yes, we can recover." None of us would like to be defined by a past when we were not at our best; we must have the freedom to learn and to grow from our experiences. And while we need not shamefully hide away unlovely truths about ourselves, we should also not get overly fixated on the faults or shortcomings of another.

This is the razor's edge, to know the whole truth of a soul's journey, and not get hung up by something negative when the bigger picture reveals a soul ascending beyond those falls on their way to spiritual perfection.

—∞∞∞—

When we are in the adventure of exploring God, in creation and beyond, and we challenge the frontiers of limitations, not accepting anything in life as being normal—in the sense of being absent of God—then the normal frontiers dissolve into something more, something greater, something Divine. For most of us, this is a process. However, it does not take much reflection to see the various ways that our minds have created barriers, even beyond our conscious intention—and that these barriers keep us separated from Sacred-awareness.

Let us journey together until we know, absolutely know, there is nothing but He, nothing but He. And, as our dear Swami Satchidanandaji said to do, "Dive deep, soar high."

—∞∞∞—

Love, is not sentimentality, but a guiding force. When you love, you will not do things that you know will bring about harm to yourself or others. When you love, you will not act out of greed, but with integrity, evoking the principle of love for one and for all.

When you pass laws and regulations, you work for the highest good of all when love is your motivation.

Whatever the form of government, legal system, and opportunities for businesses are in place, there is one immutable law that will determine the greatest happiness for the most people—the law of love. Without this guiding principle, all forms of government and legal systems are simply empty shells.

When you are in integrity with higher love, you run an honest, clean/clear business, and you feel the purity of that honesty—you are left without stains on your soul. You do not ever need to look over your shoulder for someone coming up behind you because you have cheated or lied to them. There is a fair exchange of money for goods or services: both giver and receiver benefit from this transaction. This clarity of purpose, this purity of action, is what you carry forward with you; it is a gift you have given to yourself, and to the world you interact with.

When your focus is on love, giving good service, speaking the truth, and offering kindness and compassion, and you do all this without expectation of receiving it in return, then you are saturated with the quality of love—because it has flowed through you, it blesses you. This is due to the nature of love I am speaking of: it does not emanate from you; rather, it flows through you from something greater than just you.

You punish or reward yourself, and those around you, according to the purity of your intentions. Beginning with, and carrying through with, the intention of love not only rewards you internally—it is what defines the best business practices, the best government, and the best legal system. It is not always openly displayed through talking about love, but you know when someone is acting with integrity, sincerity, and working to give the best goods and services—you naturally want to reward them with more business and recommend them to others.

—————

The story is told of the pearl divers. The pearl divers swim under the surface to find the valuable pearl. But only the divers who are willing to dive deep will discover it and know the wealth it promises. We too must learn to dive deep, to drop further down in meditation, to truly experience the greater Reality.

To merely play on the surface will never awaken this deeper superconscious life.

God is bliss, ever-new joy, shining truth, and a living awareness of the eternal nature of life—all of this awaits the pearl diver who is for God-experience—it awaits you.

—————

Just as the Divine Mother arranges for darshan, so God arranges for knowing the Divine Presence for the sincere and aspiring heart, bypassing the fierce noisiness and confusion of this world, and taking us into our inner temple of silence where Divine Mother reveals Herself.

The message comes: we should not be dissuaded by the outer fierceness of the image of Kali, or of this sometimes-harsh world, but we should dive deep into devotional meditation to find the pearl of realization that reveals the beauty of God, both within and without.

—————

Not speaking is not the real silence (it is amazing how loud and nonstop the mind can be!). Only by stilling the body and mind do we beget true stillness. Then, inner stillness is born in the heart: a place of deep connection with the Infinite Divine that is the firm foundation for oneness with God.

—∞—

The key to any society surviving and thriving is for the vast majority of people to abide by the eternal truths that all religions have taught. The central commandments of Moses, and the yamas and niyamas of Patanjali.

—∞—

Master taught us to focus on the spiritual eye, the point between the eyebrows. Since time immemorial, the spiritual eye has been known about and represented in art and lore.

Spiritual scientists discovered that this third eye point is the doorway to the Kingdom of Heaven and that, by focusing on it, we might open up this portal—we can ascend into that Kingdom, and it's Light can descend into us.

Then we realize that this world really is a dream-reality, and the Kingdom of Heaven is our real home, the truth of our being.

—∞—

Oneness is a merging into the seventh chakra at the top of the head. The tall headgear or hats used in religions are symbolic of the fully opened seventh chakra. Depictions of the Buddha show three coils of hair above the top of the head, indicating mastery over the three bodies, the physical, astral, and causal: in other words, being established in this highest center.

This is the summa cum laude for the yogi or spiritual master. Mother called this, "Going over the top." Once the individual has been completely subsumed into the spiritual, then the spiritual may once again manifest as the individual, only now it is all done in complete accordance with all the purity of the spiritual consciousness, manifesting through the human—the complete God-man or God-woman.

Whether we find ourselves on the first rung of this story or in the final mile, the pattern we follow is the same—we stay true to the higher light of truth, love, and universal service in all we think, say, and do.

Touching the hem of God makes us drop to your knees in disbelief that this divinity has been secreted away in the recesses of our Being all this time, yet we never knew it. It is then we stand in wonder as to why we took so long to make the effort, to go deeper, and to soar higher.

Now we can be with the suffering of this world; it swirls around us, but know that we are not that. I feel the sorrows, losses, pain, and misery of others deep within, yet there is a deeper knowing of Reality that shines beyond every dark cloud—and this makes all the difference. That we may all know this superior Reality, that each one's axle stays true even through life's many bumps, is my greatest thought and prayer for each one of you.

―∞―

Being immersed in the transcendent God-experience, the mind is further purified, lifted into the state of para-bhakti, the supreme state of Purushottama. The para-bhakti perceives the transcendent state manifesting as the world, the body, and even as the expression of the ego; all are manifestations of a single, unified life.

Now, God is seen operating in the highest consciousness and manifesting as all in all. In this supreme Reality, everything is known to be God—within, without, and everywhere about. Established in this supreme Reality, the soul fulfills its highest purpose.

―∞―

In Omnipresence we feel what others feel; however, it is not a simple connection to another, rather, we take with us awareness of God's love and compassion as well as His clarity that helps us discern truth and right behavior.

―∞―

When any aspirant "lifts up" the human consciousness (the son of man) into the Divine Consciousness (our Heavenly Father), the aspirant knows the same transformation, the same truth. Whatever happens to the body and the world becomes like water slipping off the "enameled leaf," leaving the inner Son of God ever in oneness with the Heavenly Father.

———<>———

It is not that simply spending more time in meditation results in progress, but there is something about extended meditations being required for going deeper. With increased time, internal operating flaws are met, and a new downloaded code allows for higher planes of consciousness. It may not always be the fact that something "incredible" occurs; rather, it may be a grounded deepened awareness in Spirit that is being established.

———<>———

God is a Reality that we may know in truth through direct inner experience.

———<>———

There is a built-in failsafe: the Savior is the Light seeded in humanity and is present in everything that is made. So, the thing is to discover that Reality—to accept deeply into our being the light of truth that has always been with us—Light is in every person walking the earth. The Light was awakened in our dear savior Jesus, even as it can become awakened in each and every one of us.

———<>———

Throughout all of this magnificent desert, vital life-force flows and animates all we see. Mountains, plants, and birds are all vibrant, and live mostly by nature's design, leaving little room for independence. When we get into the higher forms of mammals, we see more examples of will and independence, but only with the human being do we see a real development of abstract thought, self-reflection, and an independence of will that can either go seriously astray from its original design, or else, be mastered and transformed into transcendent Consciousness. Sinners and saints are almost exclusively the province of the human species.

—

I sit here, surrounded in Aum vibration, resounding within and without; life-force twinkles in walls, floor and in every material thing; the Divine Presence is blissfully thick in the air; only a spiritual awakening can open the doors to such realities. This is not my province only, but the inborn nature of us all.

Let us not live on the surface of life; let us dive deep into the Reality that Divine union alone can bring us.

—

Faith in God: that He is in charge of this universe; He has a loving, caring hand and is the mover behind all events; He turns off the fuel for fear.

—

As we deeply meditate, we will move through our own thinking world and enter into a perfect calm realm of inner stillness—"Be still, and know that I am God." It is in this still frame of mind that great Truth may emerge from our own depths of connection with God. It will come as self-evident Truth; it may shatter our own closely-held beliefs or it may confirm what we have thought previously to be true; only now, know it as pure Truth.

———

It was with the power of this Truth that Jesus was to build his church of Self-realization.

———

Purifying sexual energy on a human level means finding beauty in complimentary relationships between the sexes, the ability to transmute it into a creative force, and appreciating its sacred power to bring about new life—a truly remarkable miracle.

———

Our ascent into Divine Consciousness proves that time and timelessness are completely dependent on shifts of consciousness.

———

There are literally no barriers. Even what we call death is no bar to the power of Love. It is not sentimentality, nor is it blind or deluded, rather it is transcendent and knows the worth of another far better than what the faculties of our senses or mind can comprehend.

Whether we are practicing loving God in order to attain Him, or we are immersed in divine love through realization, love will be found to be the most potent force in all the three worlds.

To remain in a sterile world empty of emotion is not proof against suffering; it is only through union with God will we know that freedom. If we ask, "Where is this love you speak of?" It is here, within us, and all around, we are verily swimming in an ocean of love, and always have been—we need only receive it.

SEARCHING

With that Journey of journeys wide open before us, with simply the will to explore needed to do so, I stand with you, hand-in-hand, to begin ever-new the great adventure in God.

———&———

The key to gaining spiritual freedom, that is the removal of suffering, is the ability to learn from our experience. This ability to learn from experience is basic to all growth. So many people repeat the same errors and expect different results: this is insanity.

The soul who wishes to really grow must be a keen observer of cause and effect, for this is the universal law of creation.

———&———

This life does take you to so many places, in body, mind, and spirit; every one of them has great meaning in your ultimate adventure in going to God.

The key to finding happiness in the journey is to find that place of stillness within your heart and soul, and never let it go.

Then be in wonder as God unfolds His life within you and all around you; and oh, the places you will go!

———&———

Love and truth must go together, or neither can be whole.

There are facts devoid of love, but facts in and of themselves can never be truth. Facts can be used as a weapon to hurt and destroy, but this is not truth.

To know truth, you must behold not only the facts, but the soul; about which the facts are but one facet.

—∞—

Love is not always meek and mild, but it is always humble; surrendered to God. Be sure before you pronounce something as the "truth" that it has merged with love, for only then does it deserve its name.

—∞—

It is very interesting to notice not only the physical surroundings you are in, but also the subtle vibrational reality that accompanies all creation. Spiritual beauty and physical attractiveness can be at complete variance with one another, and then on some occasions they express themselves equally through some charming form.

—∞—

This is the great secret of love: the more we give, the more we receive.

If, out of fear and resentment, we do not give, then we do not receive.

—∞—

Imagination is often derided as a false reality. And, it is a fact some can imagine many things, both true and false, and call it all true. But that should not take away from the reality that imagination can create a doorway to higher Reality; imagination is not that higher Reality, but it can trigger a true experience.

––––

We all can merge thinking into Being with practice and purification, and oh, what we may become as we explore our true Being!

Can you not sense the call of freedom tugging at you like an open breeze that seeks to fill the sails of your spirit and take you into unending Bliss?

It can start with your imagining this reality unfurling those closed tight sails, but then you enter the doorway and find yourself moving into the Reality of the freedom-loving Divinity within you, and all about you. Even now, *do you not hear the call?*

––––

What is this life all about?

This is a question that makes us go deeper than just living on the surface.

This quest for meaning can be the beginning of the greatest adventure in life—the search for God-realization.

––––

Pilgrimage spots are wonderful for traveling to and becoming immersed in the uplifting vibrations to be found there: such as where sacred rivers join together.

However, in truth, everything we need to have the highest God-experience is to be found within.

—————

All should know that being married and living a householder's life is not a bar to the highest realization.

—————

Science prides itself on observing phenomena, manufacturing theories about what it sees, designing an experiment or two, and noting if the outcomes behave according to what the theory anticipates: an admirable process for physical and psychological phenomena.

However, what about Spirit that originates outside material creation?

Then the only "instrument" for measuring results is found through intuition and deep inner experience, both of whose range is beyond that of a telescope or a microscope—what then can physical science say about it?

—————

This Silken Road is the pathway to the gold of the spirit, and in our restless search for lasting happiness, it alone is the fulfillment of our heart's desire. There is both power (life-energy) and refinement (bliss) in this movement. While a value could be placed upon goods traded in days of yore on the Silk Road, the experience of God with the

Silken Road of the spine and brain is beyond compare, and thus invaluable.

⸻

When we are attuned to the inner Quiet, then the resonance of Spirit easily transfers itself to the open heart—God is everywhere speaking His truth, love, and kindness. However, it is only those who have "eyes to see, and ears to hear" that such wonders reveal themselves.

It is not difficult to perceive this sacred essence; it only takes a keen desire to know Spirit within and without—giving up prejudice of presupposition, and standing in wonderment and awe in one's own prime simplicity, that leads to such receptivity.

Such willingness is not hard, but seems to be rare for some unfathomable reason—for being blind and deaf to this miracle is a banishment that is hard for the soul to endure.

Attunement to God cannot be made up for by the constant bombardment on the brain of playing music, watching television, drinking alcohol, or taking drugs, all these things leave the soul even more thirsty for the Living Waters of pure Spirit.

⸻

Those of us who seek out God-experience have come to the conclusion that there is nothing in this world that can give complete happiness, for anything that is born must die—death, being the end of things, must necessarily take happiness with it. Therefore, only that which is eternal can give fulfillment to one's heart's desire. But eternality alone is not enough, for life without abiding joy is hell; so, ongoing bliss must be part of the equation.

The other required element that may seem self-evident, but is also necessary, is that one must be a conscious participant in this experience of eternal bliss. The combination of an eternal self, consciousness, and bliss–Sat, Chid, Ananda—must all be present for real and lasting happiness.

There are other elements, of course, such as truth—no one would be satisfied with a life based on lies—expansiveness, purity, openness, the happiness of others, connectivity, and more.

⁓

Truth means we do not distort the reality—truth goes to the heart of the matter with clarity; it is not swayed by emotion or bias.

⁓

It is a natural thing, when coming into this world without a living awareness of our larger existence, to feel that this body and this world is our all and all. However, this becomes a problem since everything here is temporary. The basis for our existence is quick and flows through an hourglass. This can only provoke anxiety on some deep, existential level, especially as we see the sand running out for ourselves or others.

The question then must be asked, "Is there no alternative?"

In my case, as with many of us, my interest took me to those who spoke of having actual experiences, of experiencing states of consciousness that positively described what, at my core, my soul needed to know. Beyond being interesting, to hear about these experiences made my soul say, "Yes!"

These are mystical experiences; that is, experiences that reach beyond the five senses and are not the product of logic, but they hold up to logical scrutiny when you accept the premise of the experience. They also have the added virtue that they are not formulaic, nor in need of accepting a creed, but are based on seeking out experience.

If science, philosophy, or the acceptance of a creed satisfies a soul, then that is sufficient. However, I needed something more—I needed to touch Truth and to experience it in such a way that my soul found complete satisfaction in the here and now.

A product of this exploration for me not only emphasized the temporary nature of life in a body, nothing great in that obvious deduction, but also it gave me experiences in what transcends transitory nature: the ever-existent Soul. During these particular experiences, I was lifted above the imprisoning limitations of normal ego-bounds and I saw and knew that "I" was never created, for I was without beginning, or end—this "knowing" was liberating beyond belief.

I saw that I existed before taking incarnation in this body and I knew that I would continue to exist after this body has returned to its natural elements. I experienced that I have always been and will always be. I found this awareness to be sublime, it filled me with an inner assurance and satisfied my soul's quest.

Collectively, we can stand up and proclaim the Truth of truths: realization is religion; there is no religion without realization; and, religion loses its most profound meaning when it fails to raise others up into the heights of realization.

With the synergistic relationship between realization and religion, the tremendous potential of humanity is unleashed.

As our great and dear Galilean Master said, "And ye shall know the truth and the truth shall make you free" (John 8:32).

Those who know God are, above all else, sincere, pure minded, and of soft heart—they continually focus on attaining the supreme state of realization—they are simple, unpretentious, and dedicated to truth.

Oftentimes, those who gurus seek to help are not able to fully take advantage of what they are given. But even though gurus want realization for all aspirants here and now, they also have the understanding that each soul comes with his or her own karma and purity of desire.

A few may fully take what is given, others, just a portion, and some may walk away empty-handed—not because it was not freely given, but because the individual was not yet ready to embark upon the Great Adventure.

―∞∞―

For those who are awakened to their spiritual purpose, there is no reason to stand in judgement of those who are seeking to fulfill more earthly goals, as long as that is their true purpose—we can take joy in seeing that other souls are seeking out what is truly theirs to do.

Just as we can affirm that, even when our soul's purpose takes us out of the common ways of this world, we are exactly where we need to be and may rightfully feel joy in knowing that we are fulfilling our true purpose.

―∞∞―

I bow to the Divine Mind that has taught us about universal symbols—unfolding their meaning so that we might all learn to soar.

―∞∞―

In the East, the dragon is in the positive, elevated state, with the power to give boons to the deserving supplicant. The dragon's ability to fly means it has uplifting power, and it also has mastery over water, which symbolizes consciousness. We see the dragon in festive array during New Year celebrations, being paraded down the street with the idea of bringing good luck for the new year.

―∞∞―

I bow to the Divine Mind that has so taught us about universal symbols—unfolding their meaning so that we might all learn to soar.

——&——

Through the bhakta's repeatedly touching the fabric of God's Being, the mind is further purified, and now the state of God-experience makes the world seem like a dream.

In this uplifted state of the jnana, the mind thinks of the world as an illusion that is not God. The jnana says, "Transcendent God alone is real; all else is false." This high state of the jnana is tremendous, but it too is not our final destination—there is more.

——&——

We must be careful that our thoughts and words comport with highest truth to promote the greatest good.

——&——

Great revelations search you out: are we receptive to the Truth that will transform us and the world in which we live into a living Christ Consciousness?

——&——

There is no greater life to live than this.

——&——

When the World Intrudes

When someone injures you through mis-behavior, see the situation as you imagine God would see it. You may think, God feels pain for everyone involved, but He is also dispassionate; God is always God. And God always sees the truth of a situation, He is not blinded by a need to gloss over a behavior.

———

You might say this is about anti-thanksgiving, those things we are not grateful for; when people lie, cheat, steal, and even murder. As aspirants for realization, what do we do when our lives are touched by, or we collide with, such situations?

———

The fear of what others think, how they might judge you, is a tyrant that never releases you from a self-made prison of what others expect and what judgements they may have.

This can come as a great test for the aspirant; not just with family but also friends, business associates, even what strangers might think of you if they knew your deep spiritual nature.

To free yourself from this prison, you must make what God thinks more important than what others think. There are times and situations that can really test your loyalty to God and to your spiritual path.

———

There are times in every aspirant's journey when doubt works into the mind and soul.

This oppositional force acts with vicious efficiency, wiping out every memory of spiritual enlightenment that had been previously experienced.

These "crisis" moments will come, and depending on what you do with them, they either act to propel you to your goal, or they become a weight that will sink you in a sea of ignorance.

Even in the lives of great avatars, storms of doubt railed against them: Rama while in the forest and separated from Sita; Jesus in the garden of Gethsemane, and Buddha during his night of testing. Doubt in your purpose, doubt in a higher reality, doubt in your teacher/guru, doubt will surround you like a dark clouded veil.

Throughout this taxing time, recognize it as a test, and despite the lack of light at such a time, faith makes you continue forward. You need not pretend to know anything you do not know, only have faith that the test is a test, and that by remaining loyal to God and guru, you will eventually pass through it.

⸺

All healing begins with love and wisdom, and healing ends with an immersion into love and wisdom.

We may protect ourselves, but let us always be guided first by love, and not retaliate with anger, for anger perpetuates an endless cycle. Rather, wisely, give love for anger for the resolution of yours, and the world's, ills.

⸺

In truth, creation has always been pure, only the clouds/ maya make it appear dark and black. Remove the veil of maya (the clouds) and all of Spirit and creation are once again seen in their innate purity.

—∞—

It is the human mind that is the battleground for these two ways of perceiving the source for overcoming—the human and the Divine. Years and lifetimes of survival mode make us think we must rely only upon our own wits and capabilities. And, although it becomes clear there is a Divine Consciousness that is the true source of our being, past programming remains strong in feeling *it is just me*.

—∞—

Build a bridge to God by thinking of the life-energy that is in the pain impulse itself; that life-energy gives the electrical impulse its power to travel to your brain via nerve pathways. By connecting to the life-energy that is behind the pain impulse and affirming that the life-energy comes from God—you are directing your mind back to its ultimate Source, and, as a result, you feel greater strength, peace, and an ability to weather any storm coming your way.

—∞—

It is clear that when God is present, then we may enjoy the world according to His will—knowing that if He is not in residence, then it all loses its value and meaning. But, being keenly aware that this is His world, that He manifests Himself in all forms, then we may know Him through His manifestations.

Lose sight of Him, and all is lost. Know Him to be the best of this world, and we may glorify Him through His manifold expressions.

In every area, total surrender to Him. In this way, we discover anew, that in seeking His kingdom and righteousness first, God gives all of these things (and more), to us as well.

There may be a time when something occurred that was outside of our control, yet the results of what happened continue to haunt us. In this case, we may recreate the situation by seeing ourselves surrounded by the Light of God—the masters are all around us, and angels of mercy hover nearby. We feel a deep, unshakable, calm within. We may see those around us also in the Light of God.

Many times, people will say and do things out of their own anxiety that land very hard on us, and they do not realize the effect it has. Other times, they do know, and feel powerful in "lording it over" another. In either case, it is done in ignorance, and they will have to suffer the pain they inflict on others.

Real healing comes in divine understanding, knowing that whatever we do to another, we do first to ourselves.

Though we may differ in ideas, we have a history of peaceful political transitions, the rule of law, and freedom to speak our minds. Let us not become so overheated that intolerance and hate supersede peaceful ways of expressing our differences.

Wise or ignorant, freedom of thought is a fundamental right from our Creator—as He proves by giving us minds that will never perfectly agree one with another. God's will is supreme, let us trust in Him to guide this world in all its ways for the highest good of all.

⎯⎯⎯⎯

Rise above the thralldom of everyday concerns—know the Supreme One, the One who is ever-present within you.

⎯⎯⎯⎯

In any transition, there are many things to do, sometimes there is a "grinding of gears" while shifting from one mode to another. It is good to be mindful of transitions in life, both small and big. Leaving, or arriving home from work is a transition, going on vacation (there are many circumstances of those going on vacation, getting sick, as if they can let down, and somehow that translates into the immune system letting down as well), then, there are those larger-life transitions, sickness and death that cause even greater ripples, and sometimes tsunamis, in life.

Through it all: breathe, be mindful, and stay connected with God so that we are ever anchored to our true Self, not swept away in the many changes that life is constantly offering us.

If we are very mindful, we will notice that even the tide of breath from in to out, and out to in, is a transition.

May we ever move into life's new situations with a calm, knowing oneness with our Heavenly Father, Divine Mother ever with us, guiding us, and giving us inner assurance that no matter the changes, all is well, all is well.

Although we may strive to maintain a positive environment to live in, we may freely admit there are many things outside of our control. We can acknowledge that if those negative things beyond our influence are given preeminence in our mind, they can bring us low.

The greatest boost to our physical, mental, and spiritual immune systems is God remembrance. Through God remembrance, the first thing that happens is that we take our mind off of the merry-go-round that makes us feel overwhelmed or powerless and we align with the supreme power and divine intelligence of God.

God is positivity itself: hope, faith, and a doorway to all things possible. Remembering the attributes of God: "Oh Lord, You are all-powerful, wisdom and light itself, You are peace and love without limit—You are my all, and all, in all."

Chanting God's name, meditating upon Him, listening to inspiring talks and music elevates our mood, changes our thinking, stimulates smooth life-energy, and purifies the mind—both our conscious and subconscious minds are uplifted through our contact with the superconscious mind.

———❧———

There are times in life when health, prosperity, work conditions, family life, and friendships can all go through transitions, sometimes going our way and other times not. And, yet, finding peace, inner assurance, a solid foundation in a constantly changing world is at the heart of our spiritual practice.

Even Mother said she could have an initial shock when something first happened. We too may feel, at first, an initial disturbance, but like a compass needle that always finds north, so our minds go directly to God. Other times, we may find no disturbance at all when something untoward happens; we simply feel the great divine peace from start to finish.

———❧———

Survive and even thrive through terribly difficult circumstances by looking for the good even when it seems that life provides nothing but hard knocks.

———❧———

While all life-events are important, they are but a tiny portion of a much greater Reality. When you think of the ocean, the waves on the ocean's surface are powerful and produce a lot of activity; still, when compared to what is occurring below the surface, there is so much more ocean below than what is seen on the surface. You soon realize that the surface is but a miniscule percentage of the whole, and while not insignificant, especially to those busy riding the waves, surface living pales in significance to the real power and life found below.

Worldly life is the wave action; the great Reality is what lies below.

—∞∞—

Change is the nature of this world. This is a simple fact. Yet there is a part of the brain that, to make sense of this world, looks to those predictable things in life to help us to find assurance and order: assurance that the world is safe, order so that we might navigate this world and find happiness. So, while certain parts of the brain are looking for order, change comes and upsets that looked for order—change that can make us feel shaken to the core.

—∞∞—

Realization can bring us to a crisis point; if the world cannot do it, and we cannot imagine anything greater than this world, then why exist? And some will take their lives. But that does not work either, because we find ourselves right back in a body, facing that moment all over again. At last, that emptiness, loneliness, and yearning for something greater, leads us to long for that "something more" above this horizontal plane of material existence.

This need takes us further than simply to an idea that there must be a heaven waiting for us at the end of life, for at that point, we cannot wait and defer for some hoped for future happiness. It is here and now: we must know the truth.

It is at this moment of realization that we really enter the path to realization.

—∞∞—

Through focusing on the third eye, and watching the breath, we suddenly feel uplifted—attuned to something higher than ordinary daily experience—in deepened meditation, and all through the day, we keep this focus.

We can cultivate the idea and feeling that the things of this world are passing phenomena. We definitely live in this world, but with this perception, we are not touched to the inner core of our Self by this changeable dream-reality.

—∞∞—

Let us live in our core, from the inside-out,—instead of how we lived in our past life, from the outside-in—outside-in is when you are defined by the body and its relationship to the world.

—∞∞—

This should not be imagined as a season-less life, that knows no ups or downs—if that were the case, then you would not be participating in life, only observing it. But you can find a place inside that is the calm center, even as events are churning all around you.

—∞∞—

Some live lives pulled along by the current of the world, doing what others do, until they come to a point where they realize that they have lived their lives according to the expectations of others. They do not really know their true purpose.

It is knowing our true Self that grounds us to timeless truth, freeing us from being not simply swept up in the time-current of the moment. The seas of our life can be stormy, and wind-tossed with crashing waves all around, or it can be open blue skies, placid, and silky smooth.

Whether we are in our ups or our downs, there is a singular spiritual Presence that is ever the same—calm, pure, steady, and always a comfort and a guide.

Time and experience teach us the superior value of being in communion with this Presence as it proves itself to be our one, true, reliable friend and guide throughout all time.

When you have challenges of health, prosperity, and relationships, inwardly commune with your infinite Beloved and give thanks, knowing He knows all that you need, and His great love and desire for your good to come to you is even now doing so.

Divine Will ordains for many spiritual masters to be subject to the vicissitudes of life in order to demonstrate how to move through life's many problems: to be an example for keeping the focus of attention on God throughout it all. Even when the body gives out, when friends betray you, and the world mounts a campaign against you, you can find, even as Master found, the inner strength to go on.

It is through such self-mastery that you learn about your own potential—to deny a spiritual masters' humanity is to negate some of their greatest lessons for you.

—⁂—

Through practiced intuition, you instantly know when the compass is pointing north to joy. And, because you now know that feeling of joy, you have the strength to resist those strong contrary attractions when they try attach themselves to you, foul your compass, and clutter your life with things that do not bring you joy.

—⁂—

Grief, pain, and the heaviness of the world can sometimes be burdens we must carry. However, in finding God as our all and all, then the Divine Presence will be with us in good times and in bad. The more we are focused on our Heavenly Father and Divine Mother, the more we will feel uplifting joy.

—⁂—

A tamasic-depression results in a loss of purpose, or not caring about what you know should be important.

On the other hand, a rajasic-dynamic life may have so many aspirations that there is no real sense for what is important, or essential—it is one massive ball of entangled ideas and energy.

Sattvic-calm purpose has clarity, and it keeps the soul grounded in practical actions that are tied to life's greater purpose.

———

Purpose is the guiding star that makes you aspire to something greater, keeps you pointed in the right direction, and helps simplify your life from being loaded down with over-activity.

———

And how do politics and spiritual living go together? In a word, carefully.

There are those who tie religion and politics closely together, saying that God is on their side and those who do not agree are evil. And others make political assertions with all the certitude of religious conviction: dissenters are seen as immoral. In both cases, anyone differing from the "party line" is beyond respectable.

There are real life consequences for decisions made in the political arena, so it is easy to see why emotions can take over, and that is especially true when there is no respect for the God in another—seeing God in another even when he or she may be in error.

—⚭—

Devotees too have widely varying perspectives on issues. Even this can lead to wonderful results. Two dear devotees are an example of this. One devotee has been a long-term activist for worker rights and the downtrodden. Another is a leader of a police force near the Canadian/ American border. There was to be a large protest at the border crossing. The policeman arrived at a planning meeting between law enforcement and the protest organizers. He was anxious about the coming protest, knowing that they can take ugly turns. When he walked into the meeting, he recognized one of the organizers on the other side, a fellow kriyaban, and activist-friend; he immediately relaxed and thought, "Everything is going to be ok." And it was.

—⚭—

We definitely know there are real-life consequences to politics. Today our airwaves are filled with raucous politics: sharp edges dueling and colliding with contrasting ideas and motivations. We are fortunate today that the majority of those sharp edges are words and not blades, guns, or worse.

—⚭—

The mystery is how the Light can shine in the darkness and it is not seen. The Vedas explain the inexplicable by the means of maya: a veil of delusion that makes creation ignorant of its own Divinity.

Maya does not alter the Eternal Substance that is God,

but it is a slight of hand that makes the darkness of creation incapable of comprehending the ever-present Light.

—∞—

During this cycle in the planet's evolution, there are times when we have seen more of the sinner than the saint. Nevertheless, the innate capacity for divinity is ever present in one and all.

—∞—

I asked God, "In creating this universe, why did You allow cruelty to be part of it when it is nothing but a joyful expression of Yourself." And what He told me, "For every such thing, it awakens its opposite." For cruelty awakens divine compassion, though not always in a moment or a day, and as divine compassion spreads over this world, cruelty will be cancelled out.

—∞—

The value of living a life centered in God is never so evident as when we face life's greatest challenges. For that is the time when having the strength that God-awareness brings with it: knowing His never-failing goodness, accepting this, and bowing to the love and peace that comes with perfect resignation to His will.

—∞—

We try to arrange life so that pain is mitigated, and pleasure is maximized, but we can never remove suffering as long as we live according to the limits of the body.

Only Supreme Truth revealed directly from our Father-God goes beyond duality's hold and has the power to resist the gates of hell (delusive ignorance). These "gate of hell" will not be able to prevail against the Supreme Truth.

One of the things we are taught by the world's great spiritual masters: this world is filled with opposites—for every high, there is a low, and with every pleasure, comes pain—and that only by attaining transcendent God-consciousness can we know a state of being that is proof against opposites. Bliss has no opposite.

There are indeed high souls incarnating, offering hope not only for material prosperity, greater peace, and harmonious living with nature, but most importantly, by first offering the basic foundation that makes all those great things sustainable going into the future: spiritual progress, both individually and collectively.

When you want to focus on God-experience and the cup of your mind is already filled with worldly concerns, then where is there room?

In order to know God, first empty your cup of the things of the world; only then do you have the room needed for contact with the Infinite.

Yogacharya David on a boat on the Ganges, Varanasi, India, 2005.

Who is Our Self?

EXPANSION

Let our eagle heart rise to the heavens and know ourselves to be spiritual dynamos who can remove mountains of suffering for ourselves and for others.

We are made in the image and likeness of the Infinite Being; this is the Truth!

—◦◦◦—

There is an important difference between a crisis that involves the ego only and a spiritual crisis. The ego looks exclusively to itself in such a crisis, becoming more self-involved by feeling sorry for itself and looking to blame others or feeling shame at its own existence. In a spiritual crisis, the self looks beyond the ego to find answers; it expands rather than contracts.

—◦◦◦—

With practice one can move from oceanic consciousness to the little pond of body consciousness without losing the freedom of the eternal Self.

—◦◦◦—

All the wonders in this magnificent world cannot match even a moment of perfection that we can have in Spirit. But even as we discover our union in Him, Spirit reveals its perfection, and in that experience, the world is also known to be perfect.

———

Words are too small to hold my meaning; however, those who receive the spirit that inspires the words will receive both words and spirit and be lifted up into higher regions of thought and spiritual consciousness.

———

By knowing our true Self, we cast off delusion's net and free ourselves from the endless cycle of gain and loss. Now we know ourselves as the ever-blissful ocean of God-consciousness.

———

This morning I entered the inner Temple of Silence, the thought of the bubble dissolving into the sea made it so. Whatever defines this part of the mind that operates in the world simply disintegrates; awareness becomes a vast ocean of consciousness. It is not an empty ocean; it is full of all life, everything that is good and pure but it has no need for activity, so it rests in the bliss and peace of itself.

———

To merge individual consciousness into absolute Divine Consciousness means that you have supreme bliss, a perfect knowing of who and what you truly are, and untold spiritual potential may express itself through you according to its will.

In essence, you are who you have always been; all false illusions have fallen away and you stand revealed as a perfect expression of God. You no longer crawl upon this mudball, the earth, as a worm making its way in darkness; you now are a shining spiritual being. Whatever you have been put through upon the way seems a very little cost compared to what you have become.

—————

God is positivity itself: hope, faith, and a doorway to all things possible.

—————

Many people live lives that are too cramped, with a consciousness that is too small and too crowded. In this tight space, tension reigns supreme—it feels like life is too much, that you are not big enough. This is in contradiction to the fact that you are truly made up of an infinite nature, in the likeness and image of God.

To counteract this cramped living style, you must move into spaciousness—where your consciousness easily accommodates expansiveness. Attuning yourself to your greater Self, you grow larger than your limited situation; you feel God-consciousness expand in you, making you know that all God is, is also available to you.

—————

Think of the power of a seed growing into a great tree, a supernova collapsing into a black hole that swallows everything that comes near it, including light, and the power that creates this fantastical universe we live in. Now, consider this same power exists in you as a Son of God in Christ Consciousness.

—∞—

The superconscious mind reveals what we call God, and God-consciousness. When this awakening occurs, what before may have been dismissed as myth, because it does not appear to belong to the surface waves of creation of the material world, suddenly takes on more than a theoretical potential; rather, it takes on a living Reality that is undeniable, powerful, and enthralling.

The old notion that the world of the five senses and what the human mind makes of this physical world, is the ultimate reality, falls away, and what is born is a vast Reality, the Reality of the tremendous ocean under the waves.

—∞—

Who we are is so much greater than the body, and the world; those who have discovered this superior reality have sought to awaken us from what they say is a material dream-reality.

—∞—

The spiritual scientist's aim is to go beyond these three bodies or states of consciousness. The physical, astral-energetic, and causal-idea bodies are seen as barriers to the entry into a supreme state of Being.

The spiritual man, or woman, can transition through the physical, astral-energetic, or causal bodies, and enter a spiritual state of Being that is beyond all three lower bodies.

Phasing out of the three bodies in meditation is necessary in order to rise above the three bodies, so to be established in the highest God-consciousness. Once that is attained, if Divine Will wishes it so, then that highest Source of all that is creates through you by actively manifesting in the three bodies.

Once we understand the symbolic meaning of the dragon, we know it is not a mythical being to pray to or petition for good things; rather, it represents an active power inside of us that can act for good or for ill, depending upon how we direct our thoughts and life-energy. With pure intention, we focus on lifting this powerful force up the spine—raising us into realms divine.

What an opportunity we have in this lifetime to not simply grovel deep In the base of the mountain, sitting in the dark, full of greed, lust, and anger. We can take wing and fly amongst angelic stars of heavenly consciousness in the bliss of our heavenly kingdom.

When the receiver of God-consciousness is switched on, we feel the pulse of Divine Life throughout all creation. We realize these spiritual rays have always been in and around us, only we did not have the eyes to see and the ears to hear.

⸺✸⸺

Oftentimes, we can think that the astral and causal realms are distant places, far removed from this material plane. However, spiritual experiences have taught me that these realities are all around—the substrata of all we see in the material world. We truly live in a magnificent creation, and we only scratch the surface of what is all around us.

⸺✸⸺

Once, I was walking through the woods when I was suddenly lifted into the causal plane. The rocks, trees, and path were the same, but I saw them as expressions of subtle, beautiful ideas; my own body was also made up of the same causal realm, a realm far more beautiful and of greater dimensions than the astral realm.

I understood that before material expression, everything exists as an idea of the Creator.

⸺✸⸺

With right attitude you merge and become one with highest consciousness, seeing God as the sole doer.

⸺✸⸺

"I AM"

The perfectness of the great "I Am," cannot be compared to anything—for it is unique perfection itself. These are the writings of a madman; mad for God, mad of God-experience. I have had to break the tethers of the known in order to chart these waters of the unknown. Having done so, I am now commanded by the same Intelligence that guides this exploration to write down these notes from beyond the Beyond.

—⁂—

This great sea is the "I Am," the great "I Am." This "I Am" knows no qualification. It brooks no variance.

Anything that needs qualification or change is not the "I Am."

Individual waves are always looking for qualifications to creation, not accepting the perfection of it all. Each one has access to the great "I Am," even as the wave stems from the sea, but his or her insistence on qualifications keeps him or her from merging into the sea.

—⁂—

Anandamayi Ma spoke to me wordlessly, "It is the same Light that manifests in all realized masters, and all realized souls experience the same God." This universalizing of truth takes away all sense of "I and mine" and leads to complete universal freedom.[4]

---

4   https://www.anandamayi.org

—∞—

Think about how all creation is an expression of the one infinite Consciousness, and that God is both the static Spirit that is in pure unity with its Self, and is the expressive Power that has brought all of Nature into being.

In truth, you and I are made in the likeness (nirguna) and image (saguna) aspects of God. We are all meant to be the one whole complete Spirit beyond creation, and the expressive power and wonder of that same Spirit in Nature.

—∞—

When Divine Consciousness is the medium there is a Supreme Intelligence directing it all, and the Presence of God is constant.

—∞—

The perfectness of the great "I Am," cannot be compared to anything—for it is unique perfection itself. These are the writings of a madman; mad for God, mad of God-experience. I have had to break the tethers of the known in order to chart these waters of the unknown. Having done so, I am now commanded by the same Intelligence that guides this exploration to write down these notes from beyond the Beyond.

—∞—

This great sea is the "I Am," the great "I Am." This "I Am" knows no qualification. It brooks no variance. Anything that needs qualification or change is not the "I Am."

Individual waves are always looking for qualifications to creation, not accepting the perfection of it all. Each one has access to the great "I Am," even as the wave stems from the sea, but his or her insistence on qualifications keeps him or her from merging into the sea.

If I exist in God's awareness eternally, then I am eternal, even if I cease to exist.

God is here. God is now.

With full awareness, the mind becomes still; the little bubble of the self dissolves and merges into the vast ocean of Consciousness. Now, pure Consciousness is known, the one without a second. This pure awareness resides in its Self: no thought, no information gathering, no reference to another; it is purna: whole and complete.

The inner meaning of Satsang is fulfilled anytime you are merged in God; then there is association through oneness with Sat: the great "I AM." How to describe what living in Him, and He in me, is like? There is only He, the Divine Consciousness that is the eternal Substance, all power and all intelligence—everything there is!

We have an eternal soul—our part of God that is not born nor does it die—it cannot be burnt, drowned, or in any way changed or corrupted. No matter the choices we make, other bad things we may have done (against ourselves or others), this pure element of divinity resides above the physical, energetic, and idea realms.

———∞———

Know that you have always been, you are now, and you will always be part of the Ancient One, the Source of all existence.

In that Consciousness you can rest—reside in the eternal Truth of the Infinite where a human life is but a flicker—God is the ever-existent Flame of Life.

———∞———

To live in divine consciousness is the greatest accomplishment of a lifetime because it does the greatest good for the individual and it has the most powerful uplifting effect upon all creation. If someone is starving, they must of course have food, and if someone is in excruciating pain, they should have some relief. But in meeting such immediate needs, a temporary solution is given to a temporary problem.

No matter how great the need is in the moment and how good it is to be able to offer relief, the deeper, longer-lasting suffering of humanity is found in the mind and soul.

Identifying this suffering is the first step in the recovery of the consciousness that leads to long term happiness.

———

The real change in leading a spiritual life is connected to an existence above this world.

For the devotee, no matter whatever happens in duality, there is an unchanging supremacy of existence whose happiness and bliss is independent of ordinary life.

This crucial difference is incorporated into the aspirant, woven into the fabric of his or her being, to fulfill the greatest potential.

———

Goodness cannot be completely eradicated, for its blood, its essence, cries out from the ground, or the sub-conscious mind. No matter how bad someone is, the opposite of good remains buried, perhaps deeply buried, but it continues to cry out.

———

To stand on the threshold of eternity and sing His song is all there is.

If my voice, my mind, and my heart cannot contain His melody, then He makes me mute and expresses Himself through the great Silence. For, He is the Way, He is the Life, He is all in all; there is nothing but He.

———

All of humanity seeks happiness, but so many seek it in this world only. A deeper analysis reveals that this world can never yield the kind of happiness we truly seek. Some will say our "reward" comes in an after-life—do not seek it here.

Mystics and yogis have asserted we have access to that "reward" right here, and right now, but not through worldly means. Spiritual happiness is bliss—to be found within, and in the present—and while it is latent in most, nevertheless, it is available to all.

—∞∞∞—

As a practitioner of this spiritual science, even now, turn your attention within, be aware of the prana vitally vibrating throughout your body.

Experience that this body is not a physical being as much as a life-energy being—not defined by the physical limits, but by its vast nature.

Bliss can fill this space, along with freedom, and a knowingness that I am part of all, and all is part of me. It is a seamless transition that is like a river moving smoothly towards the ocean.

Know that you are truly made up of God-stuff, and then be a conduit through which the same power and intelligence that creates vast worlds is now fully operating in you. Help bring this world to its next evolutionary step; discover your true underlying divinity—never more being blind to the elephant in the room.

—∞∞∞—

In Spirit, everything exists equally, without distinction of high or low or the many opposites that occupy material relationships.

―――❦―――

Whether it be one life or many lives we live, there is but one great lesson to learn; to be in a state of Self-realization that slips the grasp of time and space and weds us to the Eternal.

―――❦―――

God is in us, and we are one in God. With that awareness, a vast field of potential comes alive in us.

Each day is a discovery: What does God want for you? It is an exciting time to be alive, no matter your circumstances, because you are truly made in the likeness and image of God.

―――❦―――

Every individual soul is rooted in the Divine Essence and can never be separate—or else It would cease to live; it would no longer be.

―――❦―――

We are so used to being filled with ourselves, our thoughts, desires, fears, and habits, that we have a difficult time thinking about submitting our wills to anything or anyone else.

But that is really the point, God is not anything or anyone else—He is you and me in the deepest purest sense.

We are all made up of God-stuff; and this remarkable news has yet to be known by an unsuspecting humanity. Emmanuel—God with us—is really that, God with us in every human being!

When God took me through the three mystical crucifixions, He made it perfectly clear that I have a body, but I am not this body, and I have a mind, but I am not the mind—the Source of my existence is the eternal Spirit residing within and without.

Purusha and Prakriti

God is both personal and impersonal: the personal shows distinction, the impersonal none. God has His play, His lila, and He enjoys it. God is also unqualified Spirit, without separation, limitation—beyond time, space, and form. As He is in Himself in Spirit, and also the creative Hand manifesting as all nature—so His seemingly dual nature is within all souls—the microcosm in the macrocosm.

In Spirit, He is one, whole, complete; and in creation, He joyfully expresses Himself as varied forms in the ebb and flow of life—with all of its dramas.

―∞∞∞―

The air trembles, the earth is quiet, heaven and nature merge, and the field of infinite power and consciousness waits.

―∞∞∞―

Today—God's living Presence—makes all the difference. It enables me to rejoice in His work, and not despair; it gives me complete knowledge that this is His will, and therefore everything He is doing is enacted for the higher good of all. It most definitely proves what Papa said, *Pain and Bliss are the same*; and what Mother said, *God is life, and all life is God*. Every experience easily fits within these truths, and all contradictions are resolved in the one unifying confluence of Spirit.

We are all on our journey, and everyone must return to the Source from which we have come.

When your absorption in meditation transitions into activity in the world, then all sensory input is seen and felt as God living His life through His creation. You and all others, animate and so-called inanimate, are all part and parcel of one Divine Life.

To have the right relationship with the body, to remain mindful of keeping the body healthy, and doing what is best for its smooth functioning, is wise. There is a line, though, where we do not let the body, and its relationship with the world, take control of our life.

Affirm, "I have a body, but I am not this body," and give it its due, but no more. Let us practice finding that awareness that knows we existed before we took residence in this body, and knows we will exist long after this body has returned to dust. That while the body is important for accomplishing what we have come here to do, it is just an instrument for our use—a remarkable instrument, it is true, but just an instrument.

Modern science has an unstudied phenomenon, once it comes on the radar it will be one of those things that seems so obviously worthy of study that we will wonder

why there was no recognition of it before. This phenomenon is all around us; in fact, it is fundamental to all existence; it is the life-force existing in all creation, what the
yogis of India call, prana.

There is an elephant in the room most do not see—the
life-energy that animates all the outward manifestations
that can be seen under a microscope, a telescope, or
what is before our eyes. Those who have investigated the
interiors of consciousness clearly see this elephant, and it
is life-force.

This life-force enters the body primarily through the
base of the skull; from there, it enters the brain; there-
after, it is distributed to the body through the spine and
nervous system. These physical mechanisms are the conduits through which life-energy operates, but the underlying force and intelligence is the prana itself.

In addition to the normal functions in humankind, and
in nature, prana plays an active role in the next evolutionary step of transforming the human into the Divine.

When you create in life as God creates, you begin by
being ensconced in Spirit, then Spirit flows naturally as
creation. When creation has fulfilled its purpose, then all
form is withdrawn back into the Infinite.

The rock and stone speak to my soul; more than a poetic
muse, it is an underlying reality, both then, and now. The
earth speaks to us when we are quiet and listening; rocks,

trees, and all nature vibrate with their own consciousness—and as with all creations of our one Creator; each
part has the Divine Essence at its core. Equally, just as
every human being has individual differences, so does
every part of creation exhibit its own personality.

Walking amongst enormous rock monoliths, there
is a feeling-vibration of the eternal Spirit; relative to
a human's life, these monuments are ageless, solid, and
unmoving. Although we know that ancient nature cannot
truly embody eternity as Spirit does (for it comes and
goes as does all creation), nevertheless, these rock for-
mations communicate a timelessness through their very
core-essence.

—⁂—

Every life may be seen from its broad strokes all the way
down to its micro-moments of decisions, actions, and
revelations.

—⁂—

We are no longer practicing dispassion. We have become
dispassion itself. All that is in the ocean exists in us: the
thought-wave sense experiences, the deep diving whales
of revelation, the thermal layers of consciousness, and
broad river-currents of intuitive wisdom from God roll
over our surface and move through us.

Each is created, preserved for a time, then disappear
back into us once again.

All the while, we are ever at one with The Deep. We
know that we are the great "I Am That I Am" in the begin-
ningless, endless ocean of Self.

—∞∞∞—

Note the Deep in us—our Soul, Self, or Spirit.

Imagine that we are aware of all the different parts at play, but whatever they do or do not do, they do not alter The Deep in us—the changeless and ever-existent part of us.

—∞∞∞—

God is awakening this Reality in us—how can He not? Having realized this eternal Truth—when we act, we serve. For we only live to serve the One who is in all. Our heart pumps, thoughts flow, muscles move, and it is all an expression of the Light in us in service to the Light in all.

You are the fulfillment of the sacred scriptures.

—∞∞∞—

The building blocks of creation itself are made up of God-stuff. Electrons, protons, neutrons, and all charged particles have come from the Infinite's storehouse because something cannot come from nothing.

—∞∞∞—

There is a power, a pulsation that runs throughout all creation. When you awaken to the Divine Life, your awareness of this power grows, sometimes within as it courses through your body and your being, and sometimes outside of your body through other people, in nature, even in human-made creations.

—∞∞∞—

There is only one constant in all creation, and that is our loving Creator—the Father and Mother of all that exists.

————

Individuals known to me come to mind, a thousand thousand psychological patterns come into my awareness, clear and distinct.

From the Vedas and from Master's own lips comes the idea, "I am the wave, make me the sea." In the past, I have had a mental image of an ocean, waves rising and falling in natural rhythm, but now it comes as a visionary experience, the sea is a living consciousness.

Waves as individual souls emerge from the vast sea of consciousness, each express their unique pattern, then they submerge once again into vastness of Spirit.

This living sea has a number of qualities that defy description: it is full of life—it is smooth and all-powerful; the words are there but they somehow lack sufficient power to convey what it really is.

————

Here is the great discovery in ancient times by yogis: we can consciously access greater life-force by intelligent means. This life-force intelligence allowed yogis to exist without oxygen for long periods of time, and to either heat or cool the body to counter temperature extremes. Life-force energy is also a healing force and can be used to heal one's own body or to produce healing for others.

As it comes to light in Western science, the discovery of life-force will be one of the great "new discoveries" of all time.

As an intelligent force, prana does not just respond to your conscious use of it, but it will also guide you. In this regard, we may distinguish between two different forms of life-force. In the first case, life-force guides natural processes, the growth of plants, movement of planets, and the health of human beings, among billions of other functions in nature.

There is also Prana, we spell with a capital P. This higher, transcendent Prana is Divine Intelligence attuned to a much higher frequency of thought and energy than nature's prana.

Become conscious of prana life-energy coursing through your body as a tingling, electrical force that is necessary for all your body functions. Then, stretch your subtle senses to feel that same vital force in nature, giving life and consciousness to water, trees, and animals.

Through deep meditation, awaken awareness in your cerebrospinal system to Pranic Life-Force, the life-giving, blissful, and all-knowing Consciousness that has the capacity to lift you up into your oneness with God. Be a pioneer in this greatest of discoveries.

Physical science has yet to recognize the role of life-force that is independent of, and superior to, biochemistry. It is evident that even though we all inhabit human bodies, we eat food and breathe oxygen, yet there are vast differences in the life-force we exhibit. It can run the gambit of extraordinary physical health and vitality, emotional range, mental liveliness, all the way to spiritual illumination. Physical science can explain part of why individuals have these differences, but it cannot explain it all.

—

The dark density of matter is but a shadow of the transcendent Light. In creation light cannot exist without shadow, but the pure Light of God needs no opposite; it is Self-existent. Our eternal, true nature exists outside of dual forces. The dissatisfaction that ignorance creates must then propel us to enlightenment. Papa Ramdas tells us that the worse things look in this world, the greater will be the impetus to return to God.

There is no doubt that it is much better to stand up straight and walk to the door of Divine Consciousness in wisdom, rather than get dragged to that same door with bleeding hands and knees. But return to it we will—for the Divine is part and parcel of our nature and it cannot be forever hidden. It is true for ourselves and for all creation. So, take heart for this world; within each part is the whole of creation, and also that which is beyond creation—the supreme and infinite Creator.

—

The real solution is to realize the Divine Intention behind all the world's activities, even the bad and ugly. With this solution alone, a peace that surpasses all understanding comes into the heart and soul—a peace unshakable. Without this solution, fear and anger will corrupt the soul, making it ugly and distorted beyond the recognition of its original design by the Creator.

Even as God-consciousness can span the space of a far-reaching galaxy or even the universe itself, and then be found to be equally present in the miniscule atom, so can the Divine be in vast reaches of time, or in the eternal moment of now.

For God-consciousness is transcendent to, and immanent in, both time and space. It is the great equalizer to omniscience; the life of a flower is on equal footing with the life of a stellar system, or even a universe.

Life, as we think of it, is the soul manifesting through the three bodies: physical, astral-energetic, and causal. The purified body and mind are perfect instruments for the transcendent Divine Mind and are a blessing to ourselves and to this world. Go beyond the three realms, seek out contact with the ever-pure, eternal Self—not so we can get God to do what we want, but that we may be an expression of what God wants us to be.

God is the evolutionary force in nature and humanity, and, although uneven, and at times unlovely, this force is inexorably moving toward the enlightenment of all creation.

———◊◊◊———

There is but one Great Spirit manifesting in endless varieties of religious expression around the globe.

———◊◊◊———

The sound of Aum reverberates throughout, creation trembles with the power of the Holy Ghost, and nature's blueprints stand revealed as thought-creations of an infinitely wise and loving Creator.

Beyond this creation is pure Spirit, unadorned, unchangeable—ever as it has been—beautiful beyond words, perfect, pure, and pristine. These three aspects of God: creation, thought-forms of the Creator, and changeless Spirit beyond duality is the trinity—One as three and three in One—Father, Son, and Holy Ghost. For, the same perfection permeates all three, making them one, whole, and complete.

———◊◊◊———

Victory to The Light

This Light of Christ Consciousness has redemptive power and as souls around this world join together in this Light, the world is reborn into higher consciousness and the promise given at the time of Jesus may be fulfilled, "Peace on earth, and goodwill toward all men."

The God-seed within you is destined to stretch its limbs to the Light and merge itself into that self-same Light of God. Victory is assured by ever growing heavenwards.

Only Light can dispel darkness, only knowledge can dislodge ignorance, and only your sincere desire for God can make you know Him. Make sure you have a love affair with the Infinite, and worship your Heavenly Father-Divine Mother with all of your heart, strength, mind, and soul, and you will find the sacred Presence a loyal and constant lover that will make you qualified to be an enlightened Being.

The resounding Om–Amen attunes the mind to infinite Spirit. A vibrational quiet insulates the receptive soul from the constant restlessness of modern life.

Holding the universal vision purifies your heart, and it gives a needed boost to the one who offends against his or her own soul. Papa felt the greatest thing he could do for another is see God in him and her. Through such persistent thoughts by others, the God-nature is awakened, and, the perceiver of God's light is transformed through their continued practice of seeing God in all. Such is the power of God-aligned thoughts that this world cleaved by strife and warfare, cutoffs, and separations, may be lifted into higher Consciousness.

The Lord our God, the Lord is one! One Being, one Consciousness, one Reality that is all-pervasive and everywhere present. Let us look past the little snubs and separations and know the unifying principle that weaves this world into a oneness of beauty and light.

Intelligence Quotient (IQ) is a measurement of a person's reasoning ability, often equated with the notion: if you are intelligent and educated, then you are wise. However, there are many types of intelligence: reasoning ability and recall of a large knowledge base is just two of them. In addition to reasoning intelligence, there is emotional quotient, socialization quotient, wisdom quotient, and God quotient.

The emotional quotient is having full access to a wide range of feelings and the ability to process them as they arise; the socialization quotient is measured by the ability to connect with others, display empathy, and be a follower or a leader depending on circumstances; the wisdom quotient is knowing what is true, and discerning right action; and the God quotient is the faculty for experiencing higher Consciousness, and helping others to do the same.

―∞∞―

All humankind is equal in the sight of God, all deserve respect, dignity, and the unalienable Rights of life, liberty, and the pursuit of happiness.

―∞∞―

Is there any place that God is not? He is everywhere-present. Even in His greatest darkness—look deeper and behold His Light.

―∞∞―

Master asked: Is their Evil in the world? He had, earlier in his life, rejected the notion of evil, but an experience taught him that there was real evil, and there was a satanic force in creation beyond individual acts of meanness.

Then, through spiritual evolution, the mind becomes purified, uplifted into a consciousness of Divinity. This transformation reveals ever-new bliss, universal love, and omnipresent light, found within and without. With this illumination, a unity of Spirit is known to be behind the alternating faces of good and evil. Even actions that are normally defined as evil are seen to eventually produce enlightenment—the suffering produced by wrong actions spurring us on to seek out God Omnipresent, and/or by paying off karmic debts previously accrued. In this way, even evil is seen as part of the Divine Plan.

———∞∞———

What has always been will always be—and that "always" part is the essence of not only the individual Soul, but it is the essence of all that is. It is as if life before was a dark dream, a life lived in a cavern of shadows, and is now awakened to a world of light and color.

———∞∞———

To a computer engineer, the circuitry of a motherboard may look beautiful. However, that does not compare in the least with the beauty of the lotus-brain streaming with Light: a manifestation of the Divine Motherboard. And with inner-vision, we can also see the life-force flowing throughout the subtle body system. What elegance of design, with speeds surpassing that of electrons or even light—complete downloads at the rate of perfectly synced thought-transference.

———∞∞———

Yogacharya David and Carla, Kirkland, Washington, 1998.

Yogacharya David and Carla, Victoria, BC, 2004.

Will and Surrender

ATTACHMENT

Whether God calls us to a wandering life, or He directs us to some other, the same complete surrender is required to attune our bodies, minds, and souls, not with the lower impulses, but with the highest, most beautiful, sublime states of consciousness available to anyone.

And that is why attachment to things, persons, or the past makes us feel miserable, because we come to believe that we are bereft of those qualities once those conditions have passed. This is an illusion, a wave of the wand of maya, the delusive force of separateness.

In God-consciousness, we reclaim all that we truly are, and it is all good. Lets not be afraid to let go of those things that tie us to past experiences when it is time to let them go; affirm that they are always with us, all of that and much, much more.

———

As we know, temptations are part and parcel of the upward path to realization. Jesus went into the wilderness and was tempted, Buddha sat in his night of temptation just as he was about to attain Nirvana, Rama had times of despair during his struggle to defeat Ravanna and rescue Sita; even these great beings, these avatars, were tempted.

———

There have been those who have thought better of me than I have thought of myself, and this has awakened a higher light in me, made me choose the better path. But we can choose, through pride or arrogance, to push away the light, to respond to those around us that are also pushing away from the light. We have that freedom of choice, but oh what a price we pay for landing on the other side of that decisional hydrological apex!

—∞—

Only when you have the balance to walk out of the doorway of this body without attachment are you truly free to explore the vast infinite reaches of Divine Consciousness without fetter or limit—you are then a jivanmukta: a truly free soul.

—∞—

Anger can be one of our greatest tests upon the way up in our search for God-consciousness. Either a deep rage or a brooding discontent interferes with our connection to the Divine. When we analyze it, we come to know that anger is caused by attachment to how things *are supposed to be.*

—∞—

In our desire to continuously experience the qualities of the Divine, we must cut the binding cord of attachment. In this work of letting go, we differentiate between attachment and having an ideal. We can have the ideal that there should be no violence in this world, that everyone should work their problems out non-violently. Yet, we find ourselves in a world where violence is all too prevalent.

I have known those who are very disturbed by the violence in this world, and in their disturbance, they are livid.
Their thoughts and emotions emit violence in their rage.

How can they bring peace to this world when they
have none of it themselves?

Papa very rarely recommended the sannyas life to others; what he wants for all aspirants is perfect surrender
and non-attachment to things of the world. As Papa said,
"Sannyas is principally a state of internal detachment to
the objects of the senses. The external garb is only a sym-
bol of inner transformation."

Attachment is the ultimate cause of suffering for all
humankind; thus says Buddha, Krishna, and in so many
words, the great spiritual giants throughout time.

The easiest way to detach is by keeping your attention
on God—surrender everything at His feet. Cultivate the
notion that God is in control of everything, including your
thoughts, and the world around you. Feel that God is the
sole reality, and if He wills it, nothing can stop a thing
from happening, and if He does not, no amount of energy
will change it; all is in His Keeping.

This does not mean you do not strive, work, and fight
for a good idea that God has given you. But when you face
frustration and disappointment—you surrender yourself

to Him. This gives you the courage and strength to carry on in the face of obstacles, or the ability to accept something new, if that is what God wishes for you.

You are God's faithful servant, and whether it all goes your way or not, you are focused on fulfilling His will, listening to His direction, being a perfect instrument in His hands. This gives you perfect equanimity in good times and bad, in victory or defeat, in health or sickness—it is all He, it is all He!

It is a great secret in life: when you fully accept that God has you exactly where He wants you to be—it is perfect. You may judge it is not where you would like to be; however, you surrender to His will and then you feel His Presence—this makes an enormous difference in the quality of your life. He may destroy your dreams, disturb your plans, play with your preferences; yet, He always means well!

What at first takes an effort to surrender to, eventually works itself into a knowing-understanding that His will is always best, then you no longer have to work at surrender—rather, it is now your natural state. Such surrender is the great secret to peace and serenity in all times and places. Be it ever so!

We can all declare our freedom from ignorance, from the maya of delusion, of separation from our oneness with Divinity. Then, we must act upon that declaration of freedom, to break the chains of king-attachment. We truly are endowed with the gift of ultimate freedom from our Infinite Beloved; however, we have bound ourselves to endless rapacious desires which makes us a captive soul.

To find lasting happiness, we must rise above this world of duality, for this world will never be able to deliver it. There is a Source of serenity and joy within that cannot be eclipsed by dualism. Avatar Buddha said that life is suffering, then he gave the formulae for transcending it. Attachment to the things of this world makes us blind to this innate Source, so we must remove our full attention from this world, and through deepened meditation, become established in the ever-abiding Presence within—Nirvana.

Being established in such peace, we now have an unshakable foundation for entering into any and all circumstances of life, and the things of this world do not make us over-glad, or, over-sad—they simply are. Our real source of joy comes from our oneness with the Infinite Beloved—Sat, Chid, Ananda—eternal existence, consciousness, and bliss.

Detachment is your great ally in knowing the truth. Anger and fear—connected with blame and shame—can rule the mind. When detached, you can look at a situation coolly, without being overheated by anger and fear. You begin by watching your breath. As you observe yourself breathing, you then become aware of your body. Is it holding tension? Is fight, flight, or freeze running throughout your system?

As you breathe with all of this, you do not judge, you are simply a witness to what is. You are also aware of your thoughts. Ask: are thoughts triggering panic or rage? Breathe, be aware of your thoughts. Through the observing-self, step back from pure identification with your thoughts, emotions, and physical sensations that have been demanding all the attention.

Truth may reveal itself instantly, or it can take time for it to unfold in your mind. There may be many lurking, closely-held opinions and emotions that polarize truth away. There have been questions I have had that simmered for months, even years, then one day, quite mysteriously, one came to the front burner, and in a flash, my question was answered.

It can take time to step away from these deeply held limiting beliefs—to be detached. When you are detached, when you are calm and simple, then truth will approach you—make itself known to you.

When detached, you become quiet, still. In that still-quiet, your reasoning and intuitional minds are optimized. You open yourself to what the truth of a situation is: your thoughts slow down, your emotions are quieted, your body relaxes—these are all signs that you are successfully detaching from the dominance of body and mind.

In this state, you can open a connection to Divine Intelligence. What is the truth here? You set aside your ego-prejudice. You take the risk that truth may completely annihilate what your ego-mind would like, or who you judge to be at fault. Truth trumps opinion. This requires your surrender to something greater than yourself.

———

In the Old Testament, the snake is subtle and a source of temptation: the cause of the fall of humankind, and the eviction of man and woman from the Garden of Eden. The dragon in the West is greedy, sitting alone on a pile of gold, and if anyone challenges its riches, it defends the pile of gold with angry fire. Symbolically, this snake-dragon of the West represents the lower forces in humankind, such as greed, lust, and wrath. The dragon does nothing productive with this gold but only miserly sits on it. Fire is its aggressively destructive response to greed. There is nothing good, nothing redeeming, about this dragon.

New hope for new times—through renunciation of attachment to this world and complete surrender to the supreme Being, the Divine can shine through its perfected beings and raise this world to greater heights.

———

There are so many ways that the teachings in a scripture can apply to an aspirant. From learning the ABCs of a spiritual life: tell the truth, do not murder, show respect for others, all the way to the highest mystical meanings concerning death of the ego and the resurrection of God-consciousness.

Spiritual life means surrender in both the big events and the little ones—one strengthening the other. Some master the big decisions, but fail in the micro-moments; others do well in the day-to-day, but get tripped up by some radical change God directs. It must be all—big, little, and everything in between.

Having our happiness already in place enables us to give perfect service to this world. With our happiness in place, it is easy to detach from outcomes. It is our internal joy that now fuels our participation in life, not some hoped-for outcome or fantasy afterlife. Of course, we have goals for what to do, and what we want to have as a result, but our happiness is not dependent on such outward rewards.

As a result, we are centered in our Self, not identified with the things of the world. This detachment gives us a balance and a perspective that makes us more proficient in our activities.

Educate your mind to realize that the oppositional forces often come in the guise of a friend, but in fact, they destroy lasting happiness and bring you restlessness.

Love and care for those whom God has given to us, and all the while be free of the idea that "I am the doer," and attachment to outcomes.

Krishna told Arjuna to engage in the battle, and even if he is killed on the field, he is a spiritual success because he is doing what he had come to do. Sometimes, being in harmony with purpose collides with what others think we should be doing, and that collision may result in disappointment, hurt, and anger. This cannot be helped when we are obeying our true purpose. We may trust that when it comes to fulfilling our true purpose, it will ultimately be for everyone's highest good.

In the Mahabharata, the epic poem that includes an immense war, one of the warriors is asked, "Can you fight without anger?" This is an interesting question when the stakes are so high. He replies that he can. Only then is he allowed to enter into the fray.

Inflamed emotions such as anger, greed, revenge, and fear can all lead to adharmic behavior that not only retards the progress of an individual, but all those his or her life touches. Therefore, those called to a political life are tested on their own unique battlefield and are called upon to act with the utmost integrity—to ever abide by their highest Light and for the greatest good of all.

There are times when the pain or disturbance is excruciating, but it is all God and therefore it is all good. It is all about surrender to the Light, meaning letting go of all that keeps us from knowing our oneness with God or pure Spirit.

—∞∞—

I leave it all in His hands, I have the freedom to be imprisoned in His will, and there is nothing I would rather do, nowhere else I would rather be.

—∞∞—

In our spiritual practice, we can, and it is beneficial to, work on being dispassionate towards the things of the world. We can keep the image of being identified with the vast Deep of the ocean as a helpful mental practice. At the same time, let us be aware of the alternating waves of experiences that pass over our surface, but never distress or disturb the Deep in us.

—∞∞—

The opposite of surrender to Divine Will is a mind driven by the dictates of the body or by people and surrounding circumstances. The little self feels it does not have a choice in life when faced with the demands by the body and from social pressure.

Once again, when properly analyzed, great will power is being employed by the self to meet the cravings of the body and the expectations from others, only it chooses to please others at sacrifice to the self. You feel caught in a world of no choices; only, you will go to great lengths to do this, using a very strong will to do so.

We can expect others to fulfill us; that our work should be different and more rewarding, maybe even self-aggrandizing, life should be easier, and God-experience should come without effort. These can be secret expectations we do not give voice to, not even to ourselves; however, they work in the background of our minds and will rob us of life-energy and joy and take us out of the rhythm of life.

Discernment

Each of us stands at a crossroads of whether to go with the tendency of the world and tear down what is not good, or to take the inward path toward upward evolution; it is a decision we must make daily. In recognizing that the world in general does not support the inner path, we must make a concerted effort to break the trance the world induces in individuals and en masse.

Even as in times past, individuals have risen above the environment in which they were born, so we too may strive to go beyond the values and ideals presented to us by the world. To be a pioneer is not easy as you have no support and oftentimes opposition from those around you.

Self-awareness is the first step in making a change. You can make more of an effort at self-awareness by really observing yourself in any situation. When you evaluate that what you say, or how you say it, is not reflective of the person you want to be, then get busy and change your behavior. Make sure that your words are sweet, so just in case you have to "eat your words," well, you get the picture!

Make your goal in life for every thought, word, and action to be an expression of your highest Self, then you will not have to live with regret ever again. You are now an agent of truth, strength, and healing for yourself and for all.

———⊱⊰———

One principle is to choose joy. Absolute joy is ultimately a spiritual gift, not just "luck of the draw" or just for a fortunate few, but grace that comes to all. However, the key to having joy is to be really open to receiving it. There are many who say they want happiness, but parts of them do not believe they deserve it, or if they get it, then it will be taken from them: "So (goes the reasoning), better not to even think that happiness can be mine."

There is no stopping a determined soul, especially true when individual will is united with Divine Will!

Decide to choose joy, discard every other thought, and you open the door to grace and real joy; Bliss flows to you, of this, I am sure.

———⊱⊰———

Learning to be a keen observer of the after-effect of actions is the beginning of wisdom.

———⊱⊰———

Enter into the eternal Silence of your Soul. Make the Presence of God so essential that He is with you every moment of every day. Pierce the veil of separation and see that it is the Divine Mother's radiance behind the varied masks of creation.

———⊱⊰———

Rather than curb or kill our desire, hitch it to the highest star there is—Self-realization—not just to the little clods of earthly human desires. Let us expand and intensify our desire until it wants only God. Don't be fooled by cheap imitations but tap into the biggest desire there is. Let us reach out for Satchidananda: pure Being, Consciousness and Bliss with all of our heart, strength, mind, and soul!

———

Whatever is done cannot be done in secret: it shall be shouted from the rooftops.

———

Meditate deeply upon the important concept of jnana: discriminating between what is of God and what is not of God. Learn to go beyond the things of the body and this world; know that God is the supreme Presence that assuages all pain and ignorance and makes us know we are one with the Omniscient Lord. It is in this knowledge that we will find freedom and bliss in the Divine Presence.

———

The spiritual "rewards" I have known have come embedded in my practice itself. Communing with God brings tremendous peace and bliss; being His instrument of service in the world gives me real joy and fulfillment, and living in complete surrender to Divine Will makes me know what right action truly is.

———

You must be a careful guardian of your thoughts and feelings in order to have true freedom.

While a dark thought or feeling can erupt in a micro-second, it is likely that there has been a build-up period coming for a time—a preceding lack of intensity in your sadhana. Constant remembrance of God frees you. Forgetfulness binds you. It is a simple formula, and it determines your taking the higher road to true and lasting happiness.

———

Two seemingly opposite means of dealing with life's problems. One is to use your God-tuned will in order to overcome tremendous obstacles and the second is to surrender to God's will at all times.

———

I know I have had lifetimes of avoiding the light, and in this lifetime, I have made bad choices at times. I vividly remember the pain of those bad choices, both for myself and for others. Through the Grace of God and Guru, the flame did not die; the spark remained even in the looming darkness. It is true, I did choose the light. But better than that, for some unknowable reason, the light chose me and saved me time and again.

———

One test I would enact for myself when faced with an uncertain decision would be to visualize all the masters surrounding me: Jesus, Babaji, Lahiri Mahasaya, Sri

Yukteswarji, Master, Mother, Papa, Mataji, and Swamiji. Then I presented the situation at hand to them. What did they say? I did not avoid any of them as I did this. Many times, when looking at Mother or Sri Yukteswarji, I instantly knew I had been heading into a fool's errand. This worked very well to cut through mental justifications the ego-mind concocted for going away from the light.

—ee—

When in Glacier National Park we found a rare hydrological apex, one of three in the world (the other two being in Canada and France). At this apex, drops of rain could land within inches of one another and one would end up in the Pacific Ocean, one in the Atlantic, and the third would be swept off to the Arctic Ocean. So little distance in origin, but such a vast difference in destination. It struck me that choices we make can seem so small and insignificant at the time, and yet forces will sweep us off to such diverse outcomes.[5]

—ee—

First, we learn to discern what is higher from what is lower. By letting go of lower passions, and striving for what is uplifting we enter into an inner stillness. It is this stillness that connects us to pure Divine Consciousness— and through identification with God-consciousness, we transcend life's highs and lows. This realm of pure Being brings about peace and an inner knowing that we are

---

5   Glacier National Park, Montana.

more than the body, emotions, and thoughts—we are no longer ruled by them.

—◦◦◦—

God can seemingly interfere with all our well-made plans, but what of it! Is He not the loving hand behind everything that happens in His devotee's life? When He tells us to get off the express bus we are so happy to travel on; we are best served in listening to Him.

—◦◦◦—

I am co-creator with God, so my part is essential. However, the responsibility for how things go is not on my shoulders; it is on His. My part is to actively attune myself to His will and follow it perfectly.

—◦◦◦—

Each of us is called to obey his or her conscience of what to do and how to do it. A hero or a villain is not defined by whether one picks up a gun or stands aside, but whether the individual adheres to the highest light he or she knows.

This brings out a principle: Papa, Master, and Mother were all non-violent advocates, yet none were in complete agreement with Mahatma Gandhi's absolutist view—there are times and places where self-defense, or in defense of others, violence and war may be the right solution.

—◦◦◦—

We have been given the keys to the kingdom of heavenly happiness. We have also been given the choice as to whether to use those keys or to carry on with old patterns of misery-producing habits. There is no superior being judging us in our performance; it is simply that we are a product of the choices we make in life.

—※—

Discriminate between what uplifts, purifies, brings closeness to God, and what separates us from oneness with Him: let us serve God in all we do and in all whom we meet; love God more than the things of this world; and deeply meditate upon the supreme Being, our true Self, and we will free ourselves from the thralldom of suffering created through the ignorance of not knowing our eternal God-self.

—※—

Moral freedom, spiritual freedom, must then be the natural consequence of the great gift of liberty gained through self-government and from those who sacrificed so much. To squander our freedom on licentious behavior that results in a tyranny of bad habits shows disrespect for our Creator who has endowed us with a far-ranging freedom of Soul.

—※—

Human love of one for another has so very many variations, but a romance includes physical chemistry and deep emotions of the heart. One of the great challenges of human love is to separate chemistry (lust) from real love. Chemistry can be a powerful imitator of love, at least in the beginning. Chemistry can make you feel that you cannot live without another, that you can only think of another, and, in intimate moments, that you are merging into another. However, chemistry can be had with someone with whom you are not compatible on any other level. When the chemistry subsides, as it always does, and there is no friendship, no alignment of interests or purpose, then there is a sense of betrayal of "love."

—⊗⊗⊗—

Every aspirant knows that sexual desire is one of the great oppositional forces in their sadhana. In addition to this general battle, there is also a particular time when entering into spiritual experiences that the full power of sexual energy emerges and seeks to reassert its dominance.

Whatever latent desire-nature is present, it is now given high-octane fuel from the serpent or kundalini force. Given the powerful role sexual energy plays from the beginning to the end in our spiritual journey, we must know its proper role and be its good and faithful steward.

—⊗⊗⊗—

Some can look at that list of atrocities and problems and think, "How can there be a God?" Others can look at that same list, see how well we all do in general, how much kindness and caring there is in the world, how much healing happens daily, and think, "It is only by the Grace of God that decency is as prevalent as it is!" I, of course, come down on the side that God's Grace—always active and present—makes us yearn for a better world and desire growth.

Along with Grace is human free will, which can choose horrible actions, creating a daily testing field for right action for every individual and group. Family history, past lifetimes, and of course the environment we live in interlace their influences, both positively angelic all the way to demonic. Like the immune system fighting off toxins, germs, and viruses that threaten our health from within and without, so we need a superb mental and spiritual "immune system" to create and maintain total health and happiness.

Blaming others shows the fragile ego of someone that is aggressively finding fault in others in order to avoid personal accountability. In the prayer from Anandashram it states: "Who is to blame is not important, only, how shall we set the situation right."[6]

This is a tremendous statement, for blame is no longer a focal point; rather, the mind becomes intent on resolving an issue. Certainly, we must be able to analyze what went wrong, and that will make each person's actions clear; however, the focus is on how to set the situation right, not who did what.

The second attitude is shame. Shame can be an automatic feeling, with some, that no matter what happens, there is a deep feeling of exaggerated responsibility. Shame

---

6   www.anandashram.org

wants to hide, to put it all away. An overdeveloped sense of responsibility hampers individuals; they will not see the truth of a situation.

Shame is a distortion of truth and is therefore false. Also, the desire to hide from facts stops our learning from experience in its tracks.

Blame and shame are equally culpable for being villains in our desire to grow from every situation—they are two sides to the one ego coin and are, therefore, equally untrue.

We must be able to overcome these tendencies of mind. When similar situations occur again and again, a pattern repeating itself, we must see clearly without the prejudices of our familiar attitudes of blame and shame.

Jnana means wisdom, and more specifically, discrimination. In your spiritual practice, you must make choices along the way, and the higher up you go on the spiritual ladder of consciousness, the more discernment you need.

Use wise discernment in choosing your thoughts. Ask yourself: What is the practical effect of this thought? Does this thought keep me safer, make me more productive and happier? Or, does this thought sap my life-energy, rob me of joy, and bring me to a standstill?

Your thoughts steer your life—are you skillfully navigating toward positive goals? Or, are you getting stranded on the shoals of indecision, or mindlessly headed into storms of chaotic living?

Your thoughts are the one thing you can definitely choose; with practice, you become master of what you focus your powerful mind upon: aim to bring about only the highest-minded results.

—⁂—

Discernment is absolutely necessary as you build a life upwards—know that you must have a solid foundation and well-constructed upper stories to prepare yourself to succeed in the great quest.

—⁂—

Keeping your mind on God translates into not getting seduced by sex, greed, power, name, or fame, and the many other traps that present themselves to you as you ascend the spinal stairway.

—⁂—

When a position of authority is in our purview, then working for the highest good of all keeps us on the path of right action. Again, the Master said that according to what we are given, whether it is money, position, or authority, according to how we use that power, we may be given more, or, if it is misused—that which we have will be taken away—we are equally accountable when standing before our Heavenly Father.

—⁂—

Each one of us is to be a beneficial steward of what we have been given in this life. Taking the attitude of being a servant of the Most-High, no matter the position we hold, puts us into right relationship with power.

—∞∞∞—

The fact that we have chosen a God-centered life makes us unique, to begin with, but even with that, there are thousands of choices we make every day that determine what roads we will travel. We can live a life in which we are carried downstream by the force of what others do, or we can determine to take roads less travelled through very conscious intention.

The greatest road, we or anyone can choose, is the one that God, through His inner direction, has chosen for us. We may follow that road and its every twist and turn with the certain knowledge that it is both taking us to our ultimate destination of full realization and that the road is God Himself.

—∞∞∞—

When you have the impulse to create, seek out first the will of God in the matter. This attuning to Spirit avoids false starts, wasted energy, and wrong directions. With clarity of intention, bring the idea into clear view. Some concepts come whole and complete, all in a flash. Many ideas come in seedling form, needing encouragement and attunement to bring out the details.

For this work, a calm mind with a pure intention—not selfish or doubting—is the best encouraging soil for seed-creations. Then fertilize the seed-ideas with vibrant energy, activating your enthusiasm and positive vision. With pure intention, from the highest light, and having clarity of purpose and positive energy, take vigorous and active steps toward fulfilling your goal.

Attune your mind to the fact that this is God's work, even if it is a material goal such as manifesting prosperity (for all life comes from God). From the very beginning, through the middle parts, and all the way to its completion, God supplies all that you require to have the causal idea, the positive energy, and all you need for the accomplishment of your intention.

—∞∞—

On top of life seeming to go after the very things we want to protect, there is also the complication of knowing exactly what surrender means. In modern vocabulary, surrender oftentimes means giving in, throwing in the towel, and giving up in defeat.

When we look at the lives of great spiritual masters and saints, we see that this is obviously not what is meant, for these unstoppable personalities fight remarkable battles on the human front—persevering when the world stands against them, giving their lives in ceaseless activity, and in some instances, literally. There is no hint of becoming flaccid when it comes to standing up for truth, virtue, and God.

When you are surrendered, you experience an alignment with God that transcends the events of this world; surrender gives you a direction that is true and leads you to liberation: you know when to act, when to fight for what is true, and when to observe events unfolding. In this alignment, you experience peace and an inner assurance that God is guiding you in the myriad events of your life. You know there are no accidents in life—all situations are helping to liberate you from the tyranny of attachments.

Enacting a life of surrender to God inevitably leads you to complete union with Him, your eternal savior and liberator from ignorance, and you discover the truth of who, and what, you truly are.

⎯⎯⎯⎯

We are endowed with individual will; therefore, we can humanly choose good or evil. Through the consequences of our actions, we learn invaluable lessons. We see the results of evil, and are eventually driven to strive to go beyond this world of opposites. In this way, we see, even from a human perspective, that all is working for ultimate good.

Through our spiritual practice, we are purified to the point that the universal vision is realized—we now actively perceive God as the sole force behind all creation. When we see actions that produce pain, our hearts bleed with compassion, and we also understand that God is truly working out His will for the highest good of all.

⎯⎯⎯⎯

In the spiritual field, even as in the fields of politics, business, and psychology, there are those who come along who seek to rewrite the rules of right action, either through their public teachings, or their private behavior.

It never turns out well. These "false prophets" become a law unto themselves, and though they begin with a promise of freedom and liberation, they, and those around them, soon become ensnared in their own ignorance.

—⧉—

Live by eternal values. A wild foray into hedonism, expediency for the ego is not living by the creed: "If it feels good, do it." Such license of behavior promises easy freedom but ends in karmic jail.

—⧉—

This morning, God has been talking to me—it is very interesting, the way He does this. In the stillness of my mind, a teaching flows in as pure thought. This stream of Consciousness is clearly from above, and I am but a witness to the thoughts, pictures, and wordless-words that manifest on my mental screen.

It is an intimate union, and He tells me the most wonderful things. His expositions are often about the path to realization. With a fine scalpel of discernment, He cuts away gross and subtle falsehoods, those things that can derail us, and He reveals the Way.

—⧉—

Love demands the word "No" at times.

—⧉—

Being Self-centered, means we adhere to the highest standards. Abiding by right action, according to our reason, helps purify our mind which will then give us access to truth from intuition. Through intuition, we know what is true, not only for ourselves, but in others as well. Honing this skill, of knowing what is right action, saves us from disastrous mistakes.

Right action, or dharma, is the most efficient means forward, both in this world and spiritually.

Upon the principle of love for God, and for all those around you, hang all the laws and the teachings of prophets—this principle is so very true. We try to make up for the lack of the observance of this most basic principle by writing more and more laws, wanting social justice, but often end up "straining at gnats while swallowing camels" (Matthew 23:24, adapted). With the result that laws upon more laws oftentimes do little to help us, and, instead, bring burdens to the majority.

In Christ Consciousness, there is a more perfect union with the Divine Mind. Love and intelligence are both informed by a steady stream from the pure Mind of Father-God. The individual is practicing perfect surrender in body, mind, and soul, and the power of God flows freely through such a one.

In this stage, there is still the sense of "I and Thou," a thin but definite veil of division between human and Divine. The son of man, or human consciousness, surrenders completely to the Divine Essence and is willing to go through whatever God desires. Through these experiences in the Mystical Crucifixion, or the Battle of Kurukshetra, the veil of separation is pierced—when the process is complete, there is only knowing oneness of God.

———

In Christ Consciousness there is a more perfect union with the Divine Mind. Love and intelligence are both informed by a steady stream from the pure Mind of Father God.

The individual is practicing perfect surrender of body, mind, and soul, and the power of God flows freely through such a one; there is still the sense of "I and Thou," a thin but definite veil between human and Divine.

A spiritual guru: one who brings light into darkness. He or she can be one who teaches a more intellectual course of study. However, it is the rare person of realization that can fulfill the true role of a guru.

A realized being has risen to, and gained mastery of, the various spinal centers that represents specific levels of consciousness.

The first chakra concerns a basic quest for life and survival. Surrender of one's life in service to God, and to the God in humanity, is a means to rise above this initial level.

The second chakra brings desire for pleasure and sex instinct that is meant for the survival of the species—this is nature's way of perpetuating humanity. Humanly, we can learn to imbue this energy with love, dedication, and beauty by a husband and wife taking it out of the gross and indiscriminate nature into which it can devolve. But, that same energy can be used for the higher purpose of gaining realization and being of service to God—rather than merely fulfilling basic urges and sense satisfactions.

The transmutation of these energies is the key to attaining mastery over the second chakra or energy center.

The third chakra takes us higher on the spinal ladder, we come to the evolutionary development of individual will. Here one learns to submit our will to Divine will through spiritual dedication. Initially, an aspirant abides by spiritual laws handed down in religious traditions or through spiritual teachers. As the mind is purified, direct intuition of the Divine becomes possible, and through submission to God's direction, spiritual mastery is gained in the third chakra, or third energy center.

The fourth chakra, the heart center signifies going beyond strictly individual concerns—growing into a larger world. Humanly, it means loving another and it includes the willingness to sacrifice for others: a loved one, children, friends, or the larger world community. This center is a prime mover to Divine Love. Divine Love is experienced with the opening of the fourth chakra or fourth energy center at the heart.

The fifth chakra or fifth energy center, concerns knowing the higher truth and right conduct. Initially, this is known through a quickening of the mind that makes us know this is correct, and this is not. Submission in thought, word, and deed to this higher knowledge makes us activate dharma itself, and prepares us for even more perfect attunement to inborn dharma—direct apprehension of truth.

This attunement is our initiation for entering into the sixth chakra, otherwise known as Kutastha Chaitanya, or Christ Consciousness.

When your soul is humming in tune with Spirit, point out to yourself how real your current spiritual freedom feels. Compare this true independence to the ephemeral freedom the senses promised you. Work through mind scenarios in which the false premise of the senses leads you toward imprisonment in endless sense entanglements. Then, feel the bliss and freedom of God, and compare those superior attributes to materialistic and sensual pleasures.

You need this balance in life: to be in the still-static-state of inward calm and to be an active participant. In the stillness, you know your eternal connection with pure Spirit—God. From that oneness with God, you express God's fullness of Spirit in thought, word, and action, as you move from moment to moment in your life. That is why you put God first.

There are those whose choices lead to dark places that are neither life-affirming or growth-producing—these individuals become lost souls that may wander in self-produced kinds of hell, moving from one painful existence to another until that pain induces them to reconsider their choices and move toward the light of positive purpose inherent in all souls.

Let us take the time to really go to God to ensure the direction in which we are heading, and to confirm that the day-to-day decisions we are making are in concert with the highest light and wisdom of God.

⎯⎯∽∞∽⎯⎯

There are many journeys of a hero's nature that we experience over time. It can be a simple thing, such as telling the truth when it would seem easier or more expedient to tell a lie. Or, it can be a more difficult test, doing something that is the right thing to do, when doing so can cost a great deal.

Best to create a pattern for ourselves for when we face a difficulty and overcome fear: we do what is right whatever the potential cost. As a result, we grow stronger, and the integrity of our soul shines out. Ultimately, we are being purified by such experiences—preparing for the final mile of God-realization.

⎯⎯∽∞∽⎯⎯

In the East dragons are seen as powerful portents of good luck. However, in the West, dragons are pictured as greedy; they hole up in the base of mountains, jealously guarding their gold—both in East and West, dragons are generally thought of being snake-like with the ability to fly. These polar-opposite associations of good and bad dragons in the East and the West reflect the changing imagery of snakes from the Old to the New Testaments.

⎯⎯∽∞∽⎯⎯

I glimpse into the purpose of the divine plan for why He has brought me here. Stone and rock, tree and shrub, bird and walking-creeping-crawling creatures, all reveal that God is all in all, and that He wishes me to see and participate in the amazing mystery of all that He has created.

Time and again, He proves that not only is universal Spirit omnipotent, omnipresent, and omniscient, but He also delights in the unique signatures He inscribes on every particle of space.

———

The world may want one thing from you, but God is going in a different direction. On a human level, you may think that you should be doing one thing, like going across the field and beyond, but God wants you to do another, like turning around after going half-way.

To be fully attuned to God, you must be willing to go against this world, even go against what you humanly think are your obligations.

———

There is a simple psychological maxim: "When you find something that works for you, do more of that!" And, obviously, its opposite: "When something doesn't work, do less of it!"

Reflection and analysis are essential to creating better models of what works, and this is a good time for doing both.

———

Many of us do not take time to feel good about what we have accomplished, and so often we are focused on our mistakes. That gives too much weight to the negative. While reflection is good, it should be done with the idea of learning from experience. Obsessing on the negative only gives wrongheaded patterns of power.

Learn from your experiences, make amends where possible, and move on in a positive way. Do not make a fetish of focusing on wrong actions; let us learn to feel good about what we have done well and then do more of that!

—◦◦◦—

Oh, dearest aspirant, be counted amongst those who rise up to new heights and know the real freedom of Spirit; know a complete renewal of consciousness that has ever been a part of your deepest Being.

—◦◦◦—

To break the barrier between human and Divine is the greatest task we have before us.

—◦◦◦—

As a soul, you come into a lifetime with goals for what you want to learn and achieve. A goal may or may not rise to the elevation of purpose—purpose speaks to the reason for taking an incarnation. But purpose comes with a burden; if you do not accomplish your purpose in life, it is a terrible let down to the deepest part of who you are. Buying the latest phone may be a goal but it does not speak to your purpose. Completing a degree, establishing a business, raising children, moving the world forward in some great endeavor or attaining a high state of realization may be the kinds of things that speak to your purpose—for why you were born.

—⚭—

And for those of us not directly on this battlefield, but interested participants in the body politic. We too must act in accordance with dharma. The very same emotions that sink a politician can be a black mark on a citizen. Explosive anger, fear, and greed leave their residue on any wayward devotee.

Trust in God, compassion, and recognizing that good people can disagree, are ways to stay attuned to inward stillness and true wisdom. Master admonishes, "Wise men discuss, fools argue." Of course, all may have clear, well-defined positions, and many of us do, but keeping a proper perspective is a must for spiritual balance.

—⚭—

When we go through the successive layers of human potential during our spiritual unfoldment many temptations come to us: some as subtle as the breeze on a still day; others slam into us like a speeding dump truck. Things will happen: psychic experiences and powers of various kinds present themselves.

Even as Jesus is picturesquely portrayed as being tempted by Satan to display powers, to gain power, name, and fame in the world, so are we tempted. We may not have a man with pointed ears and all in red standing before us, but he may as well be. He stands before us with a silver platter, asking if he can interest us in any of his wares; all we need to do is bow down to him and we may take. Of course, we may even think such abilities are a sign of spiritual advancement!

Tricky devil. We must exhibit the utmost integrity and surrender all such powers, knowing that to the sincere yogi, these are detours that will take us off a cliff, not to the mountaintop.

———

With Spiritual attunement comes discernment for what is true.

———

A spiritually tuned will is sensitively aligned to the Self or God's will.

———

Will power is a fundamental part of our individuality. It can be used for noble, constructive purposes, or it can equally be used to degrade life and be so weakened that we feel that we have lost ourselves. Even when we feel helpless in life against bad habits that work against us, we are actually using great amounts of will power—only in the negative.

———

All the world looks for what is new out there, throwing away things of the past and focusing on the latest and greatest. Yet, residing right in our own beings is this tremendous source of power, light, and ever-enthralling bliss.

Focus

Attune mind and body to an inner-steady-calm—even as events are churning all around you.

Find a quiet-center place within you, be an observer and witness the play, all the while being a participant in life and playing the role you have been assigned, gives you internal balance.

Self-mastery is the freedom to move between the three-body (physical, astral, causal) awareness with ease. An intellectual may do this when he or she loses awareness of the physical body, or is only vaguely aware of it, and performs a thought experiment. A healer may be aware of life-energy as it moves through in waves or currents from the healer's body to the healed.

The path of a yogi is suited to the individuality of the practitioner. Only through deep understanding may you know for certain that you are following the highest path. Even then the notion that you will know everything in a factual sense is never true. What you do know is your absolute oneness with God.

You may take on the role of a master, a lover of God, a servant, a child, an instrument, or other such divine expressions. However, what is consistent in all of these spiritual manifestations is the experience that God is the operator of the machine; you are but the machine. Even what sort of expression you become is according to His will. In this sense, there is no free will, even though your experience is that of choosing to do His will.

Relationships such as a Father and Son, a Hand in the glove, the master and servant, have all joined and merged, one into the other. Now God and His devotee are interchangeable; it is God who has become the servant, and the servant has become God. The depth of this mystery knows no bounds.

—◦◦◦—

Pray to the Infinite for Grace so that you are so inspired that you cannot live a moment without the Divine Presence permeating your entire Being.

If you feel no urgency for these experiences, if time is passing you by and you do not have a steadily increased ardor for God, then pray with all that you are for God to awaken Himself within you.

—◦◦◦—

Surrender to God means that you are first attuning your mind to God's Mind; if there is a difference between your will and God's, then you go with what God is directing you to do rather than your own inclination.

—◦◦◦—

In perfect service, we discover one of the great secrets of living a truly successful life.

—◦◦◦—

An inner peace and a thrill of joyful bliss permeates your being; you live in total submission to Divine Will expressed through your innermost being. The fullness of this can only be known through direct experience.

Do not be left with the regret of wondering why you did not answer God's invitation. Choose it now, today, and every day as you move forward, and you will never look back with regret of any kind. You will then know the superior virtue of your inner nature.

Learning to draw our attention to the inner mind is a most wonderful and beneficial practice. It is only when we can turn within that we may contact God. At first, it is difficult because the mind is unruly and is not used to being quiet, but with practice, we will learn the wonders that are residing right inside of us.

The essential factor is that you must serve with a focus upon doing what is right, putting God's direction in the driver's seat. When you are driven by angry vitriol or seething revenge, no good can come of it. When you stand aside out of fear or tepidness, the world suffers.

Finding the right balance of calm, decisive action based upon the highest light you know, will produce the highest and best results for yourself and the world at large.

Determine to demonstrate your Arjuna (spiritual warrior) within—put God first and enter into the world to do what is right, with all your might.

Aim for non-attachment to this world and perfect comprehension of the universal vision of God. No matter your situation, whatever color clothes you wear, you will then have the orange flame of renunciation burning brightly within you; you will be purified, so that within and without there is nothing but Ram.

We must be mindful to keep ourselves in the "current" of God's will. Getting caught in the wrong current could end in staid waters of depression, or in dangerous whirlpools of swirling, endless desires, or running into downed trees of painful situations that rip us to shreds.

Sometimes, we must paddle hard to avoid a wayward current; other times, we are easily kept in the God-current by keeping our mind on Him. Really, once we find that passageway of God-awareness, it is much, much, easier than being subject to the world only.

A steady, determined mind gets more results than a brilliant mind that cannot hold any particular course.

True genius is going straight to the Goal of goals without deviation. Make God-experience as important as breathing the air, seeking out comfort, and accomplishing whatever outer journey you have embarked upon; make Him at least as important, nay, more important in your day-to-day life and you will make rapid progress toward Self-realization. You will find the fount of unending bliss and radiant light right within your own being. Be it so!

~~~

Lahiri Mahasaya said although man's ingenuity for getting himself into trouble seems unending; fortunately, Divine succor is more than equally inventive and comes to his rescue. No doubt curveballs in life present challenges; however, it need not spell defeat.

Fully concentrate on using all of your resources to rise above a situation, and demonstrate the power of Divine will, and grace, on earth.

To manifest God-consciousness is the reason you are here. Remain devoted to your infinite Beloved, and your Heavenly Father, Divine Mother, will make all things possible.

~~~

Keep your mind on God means just that, keep your attention focused on Him no matter the content of your thoughts or feelings. *There is only one power;* keep affirming this fact, feeling that all comes from Him; doing so, purifies the mind and cures its addiction to separateness.

God is the power behind every thought, word, and action; this is the absolute truth; it cannot not be! Never let this truth go and you will be brought into His holy Presence where no darkness or evil abides. All is He, all Is He; blessed Spirit, all is He!

~~~

To enter into the Divine Romance, you begin with giving, surrendering, serving, and loving. If you cannot find it in you to know how to do these things, then pray to your Infinite Beloved to show you how. If you stand back in indifference or fear, then you are withholding—with predictable results.

Love can only be known through free-will; love can never be compulsory.

Stand on the threshold of a new beginning, and even now, you may enrich the patina of your Divine Romance and explore the infinite nature of your Beloved by stepping through that doorway.

—oooo—

Keeping the utmost integrity in thought, word, and deed is your greatest ally as a devotee. When you feel sex-energy stimulated (outside of marriage), avoid the situation, go deeper into prayer and communion with your infinite Beloved. Surrender this impulse at the feet of the Lord and visualize the energy flowing up from the base of the spine into the higher centers of the heart, the ajna (the third eye), and the sahaswara (the crown of the head). This shifts your spiritual practice from any sort of crude form of repression to that of the transmuted energy.

Teach yourself to appreciate the superior experience of spiritual purity and freedom. Instruct the mind and desire nature, "Oh mind, observe, see how the energy flowing up the spine leads to bliss, expansiveness, and freedom. Contrast that to how confining, demanding, and ultimately unfulfilling it is when I give into it." Sexual energy is like a snowball at the top of the hill; if you stop it immediately at its beginning, you can more easily master it. But, if you give into it, it starts rolling down the hill, and when you try stopping it after it has become as big as a house, you will be hard pressed to change it—however, a strong determination, backed by divine will, can move mountains and change the course of a runaway snowball!

Higher human evolution loses connection with natural regulation; many times, the higher the intelligence, the more cunning and dominant sexual desire can be. To recognize how powerful, pervasive, and destructive sexual energy can be is not to say it is all-powerful, but to recognize its importance and how demanding of a task it is to purify and transmute it.

You can think of our mission as twofold; one is purifying sexual energy on a human level, and the second is to raise and transmute it into a wholly new paradigm—the super fuel for Divine Consciousness.

Physical activity done in service and the practice of wise discernment, by themselves, are not enough to take you all the way. When lifted into the highest centers of consciousness, you focus on one thing, the Goal of goals—consummation in samadhi by ultimate Love.

Krishna stated that extra-ordinary powers are pitfalls for real aspirants. Mother taught, "Keep your mind on God." A statement so plain that you may not comprehend its full significance until you are well along on the path.

Your life is "right sized" for you, you need only open yourself to all that God wishes to manifest through you. Let go of fear, resentment, limiting beliefs, and know that your infinite Beloved is, even right now, actively manifesting all that you need to be in His likeness, and His image.

Starting a new year is a wonderful time to calibrate all three of these parts of your life: the mechanics of daily activities, achieving those goals that are important, and never losing sight of what is essential. Missing, or mis-aligning, any one of these three parts will lead to suffering, while having all three in sync makes you know that you are on track with why you are here; it also makes you know that with your sincere efforts and God's Grace, all success is open to you for the fulfillment of your purpose, just as God has designed it for you.

In the thought of your perfect alignment with your true purpose, I wish you all that you have come to accomplish.

Keep your mind on God. You do not need to believe in reincarnation; you do not even need to know who God is—you do not need to worry about so many of the things taught, but you do need to learn to focus your mind.

—⟨∞⟩—

Good Friday is the apex of Christ's—and humanity's—existence. In the Garden of Gethsemane came his ultimate surrender. Although throughout his life he lived in surrender to His Heavenly Father, on that fated, darkest night, he found himself in the depths of despair—his angst was a moment of tremendous spiritual crisis at which time he gave all that he had, and all that he was. In that moment, he triggered the Mystical Crucifixion in which all separation from God was to be effaced; no longer would there be any sense of self, but only oneness—only God.

We too must surrender our all; we too must traverse Gardens—from the barred gates of Eden to Gethsemane's "Not my will, but Thine" (Luke 2:42),—from being a separated human, to ultimate Divine Union.

—⟨∞⟩—

As an aspirant, you must work and strive with all of your heart, mind, and will; moreover, you must hold the highest standards ever before you.

—⟨∞⟩—

The wise make straight the way of the Lord; the wise do not look left or right, but ever strive and ultimately achieve the purity of the highest realization.

—⟨∞⟩—

A frontier is the limit or boundary of an area or nation; mentally, it is the extreme limit of understanding, and in meditation, we have a frontier, that is where we meet the limit and we allow ourselves to surrender to God.

For us to continue to make progress in deepening meditation, we must face the inner frontiers that act as resistance: resistance being the self-imposed boundaries created by the ego-mind.

—ᴥ—

When I see others jump in with both feet, do the work, make God first with everything they have, I stand in admiration and awe. I know that the results will come, that that one is standing on the cusp of something great.

—ᴥ—

Here is the good news: you may save yourself depths of despair by going to God now. Turn your attention to Him, in good times and in tough times. If illness creeps up on you, if pain of sorrow seeks to enfold you in its wings of separateness, if financial misfortunes weigh you down, if relationships betray you—then take God with you.

Under stress, we tend to close down. Do the opposite—open up to God. Breathe, open; allow the Divine Current to flow into you; allow the Divine Presence to glow within. Let go of the world, all things of time and space, all outer realities, and focus on God alone.

—ᴥ—

The Vedas say, "Arise, Awake!" When all we have is taken from us, then we must turn to God as our refuge, solace, comforter, and guide. To not do so is to slide into darkness. Even then, much darkness will eventually serve to awaken the Divine within—only, how much suffering occurs between slipping into darkness and doing the hard work of extracting ourselves from the deep well into which we have fallen?

———❧———

The key to maintaining our balance is the intensity of our practice—it has to meet or exceed the intensity of worldly demands.

———❧———

To find the sweet spot in which you are energized for higher achievements but avoid a self-beating, you must pay attention to when you cross that line into self-castigation. This requires being a skillful learner balancing capabilities and abilities.

———❧———

The ideal is to be simple, sincere, dedicated, and strive for your higher ideals; while all the time being a learning machine—becoming more skillful in living up to those ideals with determination and a positive focus that allows you to grow in amazing ways.

———❧———

Every soul has taken incarnation with purpose—its intention for ways to live, grow, and learn. If any one of us becomes divorced from his or her purpose, then a crisis is induced—it may be a full-scale, life-threatening crisis, or a simmering undertow that is a drag on energies and our sense of fulfillment.

———

Artists, healers, and musicians are often aware, to some degree, of life-trons and are inspired by their astral body and the use of life-energy.

Einstein was famous for stopping in the middle of doing something and phasing out of the material realm and into a thought-field wherein he performed a thought experiment—oftentimes, to the bewilderment of those around him.

———

One does not usually need training to focus on the physical plane of consciousness, for this is the ordinary state of most people on the planet. When someone wishes to learn to meditate, he or she is challenged with memories and projections of the mind from this material plane as daydreams. Suddenly, they are thinking of what happened before and what may happen in the future in this world.

Master spoke of the ability to concentrate and that concentration is required for success in any field of endeavor. One may learn to concentrate on any subject of study, and when concentration is used to focus on God, it is called meditation.

God creates in us, and we feel a stirring when something new is coming forward.

New beginnings are exciting times of discovery, a fresh energy coming into life. Some people hold back from new beginnings because they are threatened by the status quo, but this blocks the renewal of life—fear becomes a terrible denial of life.

Some are good at beginnings, but are not steady in cultivating that new growth, unable to sustain the energy over time that is required to bring the creation to fruition. Drawing upon inner strength and determination, we can overcome all obstacles and bring the creation to its natural completion.

In harvest, we celebrate and taste the fruit of creation—we feel the fulfilment of what has been brought about. Some do not take the time for this acknowledgement and celebration but are busy, off to the next thing.

It is important to take the time, even as God does after each stage of creation. He stands back and says, "It is good." Then comes wintertime rest, deepening contact with God in the still-state, drawing from the all-powerful Spirit, renewing our soul, and preparing ourselves spiritually for a new season—to dream new dreams.

St. George subdues his dragon; he does not kill it but is pictured with his spear projecting up above its mouth. This has important meaning. St. George has mastered the lower forces of lust, greed, and anger; the spear represents the spine, with the lower energies channeled upward to the higher centers.

In the New Testament, Jesus refers to the serpent as wise and that it must be lifted up—even as Moses in the wilderness (John 3:14), St. George has accomplished this difficult task.

—&c&—

Oh Ram, Oh Lord, You alone know the ins and outs of Your plan; You alone can know what You are creating and why. I know that You only do good. So, in being in You, Your will brings about the highest good for all. Meanwhile, each moment, is lived in You, and is keeping Your will—that is what I know.

—&c&—

Focus on that joyful-bliss that is less contingent on your outer world and streams from your inner world—your connection with God.

—&c&—

Be a perfect instrument for God in thought, word, and action—to be in keeping with His will every moment of every day. This, you might say, is our meta-purpose in life—polestars that keep us tremendously enthusiastic about life and in forward motion, rising to higher levels every day—it does not get better than that.

—&c&—

I focus on one day at a time, one moment at a time, one victory at a time. That is all that we have or will ever have when we focus on Him—we feel time and space spread out into all eternity. I have a body, but I am not this body: I have a mind, but I am not this mind. I remain in the Eternal Spirit of God: the one sole Reality.

To breathe, to focus on the ajna, and to surrender the results to God, brings calm, stops catastrophic thinking, halts thoughts of disaster, loss, and embarrassment. We have to take ourselves in hand and really go to work to change our thoughts if we want to see real results.

We are not passive participants; we are actively attuning our thoughts, words, and actions to Divine Will. We are His instrument and we feel joy at His movement through us. In fact, we are so focused on doing His moment to moment will that fear is now in the distant past.

God takes us on many adventures in this life, each with their own nuances and for its own particular purpose. To accept it as His will gives us a tremendous advantage in life—for learning and for healing. This is due to the positive, determined, attitude God engenders in us that makes us more available for expansiveness—instead of collapsing back into ourselves into a condensed black hole of ego-self.

In an oceanic mind, a tremendous Truth may rise up and leave barely a ripple, but the power of that Truth will move throughout all creation. We cannot demand the appearance of such Truth, but we can ready our soul to be receptive to it.

GROWING INWARD

The heart center signifies going beyond strictly individual concerns and growing into a larger world. Humanly, it means loving another and the willingness to sacrifice for others, a loved one, children, friends, or the larger world community: this center is a primer to Divine Love.

Divine Love is experienced with the opening of the fourth chakra at the heart. There, Divine Love flows out to one and all in an unfettered way.

The experience of Divine Love is purifying in itself and prepares the aspirant to give oneself, heart and soul, to Divine Love—transcending the personal/individual and entering the impersonal/transcendent.

I am looking out on desert hills and desert expanse. It is here He wants me to be, and it is here that I am to fulfill His will. I am steeped in His Presence, His power, His glory, His bliss, and the Light of His Being. Oh, what a mysterious life He has given me.

Sense this potential—God is in us, and we are in God. With that awareness, a vast field of potential comes alive in us, so let us not sell ourselves short.

Feel that God is coming alive in us and that we do not know all that we can be.

———

Let us close our eyes, merge our little selves into the ever-expansive and ever-new pure Spirit that our souls yearn to be.

———

When Krishna revealed his universal form to Arjuna, it was awe-inspiring and eventually became overwhelming; Arjuna was not yet ready to remain in the universal vision.

You must surrender all that you think you understand about life at the feet of the Infinite, good and bad, high and low, and become totally open to the mind of God. It is then the mirror of your mind may be so perfectly clear that it reflects only your Divine Nature; only then may you be truly free!

———

Divine Mother uses the circumstances you are placed in order to create what you are meant to become. In this transformation, you can certainly feel that the heat and pressure are all too much; however, that is because you do not really know what the end product is to be. If the pressure feels like you are buried 100 miles under the earth, and temperatures are soaring to unimaginable heights, then you can only know that what is being produced will be of tremendous strength, hardness, and durability.

———

We know this prana through the awakened faculties in the spine and brain; in these times these faculties are usually dormant in human beings. Guidance gained through intuitive perception of higher consciousness is of a much greater order; it is an expression of Divine Will. Through merging human will with Divine Will, prana forms the basis for the next stage of evolution. This is referred to as the transformation of the human into the Divine.

The focus on the past and the future can absolutely rob us of the present. God-experience occurs only in the present; it also heals us of past trauma—anticipate being wrapped in the Divine Presence, always.

God-experience places both future and past into their right perspective and gives us the great joy of living in the present.

There is no doubt that as stupendous as this material creation is—it being far beyond what any of us can know through these five senses—the inner spiritual nature is just that much more. The power of it, the intuitive perception it opens, the satisfaction it provides, the fulfillment of all the heart's desires, all of these things make it vastly superior to anything this world, or numberless other world's beyond, can provide.

Attunement to God's will makes all actions taken by the devotee for the highest good of all.

—∞—

At one time in life, getting up from meditation would mean the end of this blissful music of the Infinite, but now all life is a varied part of the Creator's composition—an orchestrated explosion of the Holy Ghost.

Oh stalwart brothers and sisters, followers of the Silken Road, know the kingdom of heaven that is only to be found within, experience the bliss supreme of life within and without as an unending symphony of His glorious presence.

—∞—

Wordless Prayer does not necessarily mean you will not have any words that accompany the prayer, only that they are not necessary, and that words are not the primary means of communication. Some words may spontaneously arise in your mind, reflecting what was previously wordless, but primarily, it is direct consciousness-to-consciousness connection as God sends His power through you, His conduit.

His work being done through you lifts you even more closely into Him and His kingdom—He delights in using you in this way, even as you delight in being used.

—∞—

I awaken during the night of the full moon with God-activity so strong that I felt to be a but a small hut with an elephant inside moving back and forth! "Oh Lord, must I remind you that this body is small? You are immense! With a touch of your finger, You make worlds tremble! If it is Your wish to break apart this 'temple not made with hands,' then so be it. But if You wish me to serve longer, then You must make me stronger, or perhaps remember to use a gentler touch. Either way, Your will be done!"

From that seedling moment of turning to God when we have emptied ourselves, we will grow into the full realization of His holy Presence at all times and in all places. We see the connection then that, even in difficulties, perhaps especially in hardships, we have the opportunity to make great spiritual progress.

With the opening of my heart center, I began to comprehend its meaning—in part, loving God was opening my heart to Him, allowing Divine Love full and unfettered access to the deepest recesses of my Being. As God pours His love through my heart, He loves all creation through me; He also loves me, and in that great outpouring, love comes full circle, and I love God even more greatly.

To perceive the Great Spirit as all-pervasive is an astounding gift for any who know it now. Although we use the gifts of nature for our food, habitation, and depend on it for life itself, it deepens our life-experience to see nature as something more than something to exploit, kill, or tame.

May generations to come find that they can rest in, enjoy, and find spiritual nurturance from pristine nature—cathedrals made of stone, tall trees, flowing rivers, and cool lakes.

When you learn to surrender, to give your all, then the floodgates open and you receive the infinite nature of God—unending love, ever-new bliss, life, wisdom thoughts, expansive consciousness, and unending gifts of Spirit.

Now, as you receive, so you give. You give all that God gives to you back to God, God as Spirit, God as creation.

The more you give, the more you receive; the more you receive, the more you give. The patina of Spirit grows and glows, and you are infinitely enriched as God gives to God.

You give without thought of what you will receive, only knowing that it is God giving through you, and you giving back to God in whatever way He directs.

Real happiness is to be found within and is not dependent upon outer conditions. If happiness is thought to stem from something that is temporary, and what in this world is not temporary, then happiness will always be followed by pain when that temporary situation changes.

This understanding makes us know that only by finding an unshakable source of happiness within, one that transcends the things of time and space, will make for a solution to suffering. Great saints and spiritual masters who have gone into the laboratories of their own deepened experience tell us that there is an eternal fount of joy and bliss to be found within.

This fount does not run dry, is not dependent upon outer conditions, and makes us know the truth of who and what we truly are. This truth is known through direct experience–it is portable, going with us wherever we go, and it transcends the limited human mind.

Divine Union is the consequence of total surrender and leaves behind all spiritual practices when lover and Beloved merge and become One.

In spaciousness, breathe freedom and know that God is the solution to every problem and that His ingenuity for solving problems is even greater than yours for creating them!

There is plenty of room for you to breathe, live your life, and be exactly who God designed you to be.

Human and Divine have their own ways of seeing this world, and while they are fundamentally different perspectives, they need not clash but can work together to make up the whole—a loving, compassionate, humanity, working for good to overcome darkness and evil propensity, bringing forth a Divine perspective that knows that Good is the "first-born" of all creation, and even now, creation is perfect exactly as it is.

Thus, the world and heaven, human and Divine, are with us in the present, and our purified vision reveals that all the world is gradually evolving toward God, and is even now a perfect expression of the purity that is God.

—⚬⚬⚬—

This is what mystics and yogis have claimed: in stilling the human mind you can be illumined with the way of knowing things even as God does.

—⚬⚬⚬—

When, through deepened meditation, and a purified consciousness, we touch the fabric of God, we open to an infinite field of possibilities. Outwardly, our life may look much the same; inwardly, we are transformed. We now know that the Lord of the universe resides in our heart; a fountain of bliss is ever playing through our spine and brain; universal love flows through our heart; and wisdom-thoughts illumine our mind—in short, we have all that our heart truly ever longed for. This makes each moment a crux in our life because through our divine contact, all possibilities reside in us—there can be nothing ordinary or humdrum in our life ever again.

—⚬⚬⚬—

It is most common, when in attempting to enter silence, that we are aware of how un-silent we are! Let us use our mind's ability to conjure images of being in the quiet of a snowy paradise, or entering into the precincts of an ancient temple and sitting at the feet of a venerable saint—let our mind rest in those peaceful surroundings, being fully aware, but very still. Let that quiet saturate our soul, nurture us in peace. Simply reside there—no place to go, nothing to do, just be in the stillness.

—∞—

As Mother said: "This world is made up of individuals, and as individuals change, so does the world."

We should not look to some grand scheme of a savior from above, but to the universal Savior within. All the laws from all the prophets hang upon what are ultimately deeply-held spiritual principles, and when a significant number of individuals act accordingly, this world will be a haven of peace, where the lion lies down with the lamb in total harmony.

—∞—

It seems that within any one life, we live many lifetimes, seemingly not only distinct chapters in a life, but entirely separate books. Abrupt changes, intense situations, and altered consciousness can make for radical chapters, book endings, or beginnings in an unfolding life.

—∞—

Swami Ramdas, Papa, assures us that for everything that goes wrong, we are brought closer to surrender. It is only when we come to that point of complete surrender that we enter into total union with the Infinite.

So, suffering brings us to realization, and realization is the cure to suffering.

Surely, this is true for all life—to be in His all-powerful grip, acting according to His will, is to live as God truly meant His disciples to live.

———

The life of Jesus is replete with examples of manifesting God's will for healing and abundance, and also for accepting what is, in total surrender to the Supreme One's will—each according to its own season.

———

Whether claiming your right as a lawful recipient of all that is God's, or being in complete surrender to His will, let your heart be at peace; feel the Divine Presence full to overflowing within and without.

———

The human way is to question why a seemingly untoward thing is happening. Fear and anger can run rampant with a consequent feeling of being cut off from God, the Source of all virtue and right action.

God does not pull the rug out from underneath us, so to speak, simply to vex us, nor is it a mechanistic universe that does all without thought or caring.

If our eye of intuition is opened to the universal vision, and we see a glowing intelligence behind all life, and we see demonstrated before us His Grace operating in and around us, we undergo a marvelous transformation in which we know that we are never alone, without direction, and never without the strength to meet life's challenges.

—∞∞—

Meditation is at the core of our spiritual practice. While there are many benefits to this practice, its ultimate goal: helping us become established in the Self has been of enormous value.

The Self remains unmoved in a world of constant change. This un-movability keeps the changeable/reactive self-rooted in the immutable core of our Being. As a result, there is no wasted energy transferred into fear and uncertainty. Rather, the mind is focused on what needs to happen now.

—∞∞—

Recognizing how powerful your will is—even when used for ends that do not serve you well—can be the beginning of "owning" your will. Then, it is a matter of going to the roots of your will power and learn to direct it to positive ends.

—∞∞—

To experience God beyond an occasional moment of grace, we must deeply meditate, and it cannot be simply putting in time, we must actively touch the fabric of that which is God—experience His uplifting Presence, peace, bliss, and wisdom. Through this touch, we are transformed until we are a fit instrument for unbroken Divine Consciousness.

—∞∞—

Through continued sadhana, we experience a momentous shift in awareness: we are no longer imagining The Deep, we become identified with it. We actively see the things of the world playing on the surface of our consciousness, each part having its time of existence, but not altering The Deep in us.

—∞∞—

To find a quiet-center-place within you, to be an observer and a witness to the play, all the while being a participant in life and playing the role you have been assigned, gives you internal balance. This quiet in the storm connects with your breath and the heart. Anxiousness and desire-nature disturbs this equilibrium; hence, your task is to learn to attune mind and body to an inner-steady-calm.

—∞∞—

Experiences with solar and lunar influences have included an awareness of the full moon effect. I have an increase of energy during full moon cycles. This, by the way, is always a positive influence, waking me up earlier in the morning and keeping me up later at night to meditate—the energy provides a spiritual uplift. And when the earth makes its way around the sun and we approach Winter Solstice, I am aware of powerful forces at work.

For many years, this had stirred up difficult psychological thoughts and moods. At some point—some years ago now—those difficult moods left, and now I only experience these forces as uplifting currents. A third area I have been aware of is the sense that, when either events proceed with extraordinary smoothness, like all the skids are greased, or it is like fighting uphill all the way, it is as if the stars have taken on a helpful or a difficult turn.

There are those times when what was difficult suddenly changes, like a magnet flipping its polar ends, and what was repelling before is now easy. There may be other explanations for this experience, but I have a sense that the stars certainly seem to figure into these shifting winds.

The Work

This practice of Kriya Yoga awakens the practitioner to the reality that they are made up of life-energy, and further, an even more refined understanding leads the practitioner to an even subtler reality—all life-energy is Divine in nature, ringing out with qualities of bliss, peace, universal love, and light. Fortunately, we do not need to wait for the snail-like pace of physical science to discover all of this. We can explore these frontiers today in the laboratories of our own experience.

———

Through Kriya Yoga, we are given the highest teachings to attain awakened spiritual enlightenment because we develop the higher centers of consciousness in the spine and the brain.

———

As we eye this new year, let us not simply list those things we wish to change, as we have listed in previous years. Create a solid plan with behavioral benchmarks. Be determined to apply the spiritual principles we have been taught and let us become master of ourselves. Do not allow another year to go by treading water only: soar in the skies!

This re-union of soul and Spirit, after so long living in the Great Divorce from God, is the theme for this lifetime. All great myths, stories, and scriptures expressed throughout the world, and down through all time, come to one central point: to find the resolution of suffering; it is the real work we are here to do.

———∞∞∞———

A life unexamined is bound to repeat errors ad infinitum until there is some regard for learning from experience.

———∞∞∞———

While it is my part to strive to accomplish all that He has given me, and believe me it is the utmost importance to me that I do so, still, it is according to His will. Through His Omnipotence, Omniscience, and Omnipresence, He will accomplish all that He has set out to do; of that, there is no doubt.

My part is to willingly, full-heartedly, and mindfully, live each day as His instrument. That is all I can do, that is what He needs from me, and He will to see the rest.

———∞∞∞———

Prayag means place of offering; it is the place at the ajna where you offer yourself and all that you call your own at the feet of God. In this complete surrender, you qualify to become one with pure Divinity. It is here that your entire spiritual practice and pilgrimage in life finds fulfillment. By repeatedly subsuming all that you are into the oceanic bliss of God, you are purified of every limitation. It is God Himself who takes you by the hand and makes you a fit offering for this rite of total transformation.

———∞∞∞———

An invitation comes directly from the Infinite, "Come, come on this greatest of adventures, the exploration of your own Spiritual Nature."

Answering this invitation does require something from you; actually, it requires everything from you. You must be completely dedicated and surrendered to Divine Will.

———

Everything in the future will improve if you are making a spiritual effort now.

Master Paramhansa Yogananda poetically summarized his life of devotion and realization in the words, *God, God, God.* And Mother encapsulated all spiritual practice with the teaching, *keep your mind on God.*

———

God simply takes me to one place or another in order to fulfill some tasks He has assigned to me—as He is always working through me. Even though on the outside there may be few signs of the tremendous labor that He performs through this form, I am witness to what He does and am cognizant of the price this form pays for the privilege of service to Him.

———

From the three stages of the crucifixion, we must follow another three for the resurrection. "Touch me not," means we must rise—and not fall back into separateness by temptation of body or mind. Continued surrender, and perfect love for God, must be enacted—eschewing all attachment to this world until the work is complete.

—✳︎—

The inner or Mystical Crucifixion is a specific set of experiences everyone can expect to go through in their own spiritual ascent when the time is right.

Resurrection occurs after the soul has gone through the crucifixion experiences necessary to purify body, mind, and soul.

—✳︎—

In challenging times or in smooth sailings these worldly occupations make it a necessity to have a highly focused sadhana-practice.

—✳︎—

Purpose does not necessarily mean something lofty, or otherworldly. For many coming into this life, purpose is very down to earth.

—✳︎—

Knowing and living out our life purpose does not mean there are no challenges; quite often, it is just the opposite. A clear purpose may intentionally put us into situations that stretch us to the utmost, but we are exactly where we are meant to be. Nor does it mean that, from a worldly standpoint, we are an outstanding success.

—✳︎—

Every morning and night spent in the laboratory of my own body and soul, I learn to explore inner depths and heights of consciousness, feeling deepening peace, inner stillness, and a growing awareness of the Divine Presence.

———∞———

When you see discord and inharmony in this world, even cruelty, let it awaken compassionate love in you and then be even more determined to be a bearer of Light and Love.

As each of us do this it will gain a collective strength and one day will result in cruelty being something only known in the history books. Until that day comes you are called upon to be warriors of compassion.

———∞———

Take challenges, not as limitations, but as starting points.

———∞———

As the Master Jesus gathered his disciples to himself, he was bringing constituent parts of the whole of humankind together and revealing higher Truth to them so that they would become active conduits for realized thought and service to this world—bringing Christ Consciousness to the individual first, and then to greater humankind. Jesus' work continues to this day in all sincere devotees of Truth.

———∞———

A giant leap forward comes in uniting individual will with the supreme Creator's will, which makes all things possible. Light is stronger than the dark, love more powerful than fear, omniscience true and separation false; in all ways, the Presence of God is superior to anything this world offers.

For many people, surrender means defeat, but not for the devotee of God. For the devotee, surrender means being in the loving care of a most beneficent God who will see to it that every part of life is fulfilled for the highest good of all.

I stand in that Light and rejoice over the opportunity to live life to its fullest, to be His servant every moment of every day, and surrender my life at His sacred feet.

My Dearest One, When the world does not fulfill us, then we must turn our attention to God as our all and all. By staying focused on the world, we look to see how it falls short of our expectations and then we feel sad, lonely, and betrayed. This is a burden and an expectation the world cannot fulfill.

So, put aside the things of this world—take your grief to God and surrender it at His feet.

Oh Lord, if You will not fill my heart by those around me, then fulfill me by pouring your Self directly into my heart and soul. Be the balm of Spirit that heals my lacerated Soul. Only You can make me feel whole.

You have put me on this Spiritual Journey of oneness, and only You can make my happiness complete. I cancel my expectations for this world that I have carried for so long and I give myself to You—heart, mind, and Soul.

Spiritually, free yourself from this burden. It is the material mind that thinks, "If I only had a different situation, then I would be happy." But, is it so? God is with you in infinite Joy—why not find Him here and now? With eternal love and blessings, David

---

Know God's presence from beginning to end. This makes all the difference.

Yogacharya David: A yogi sitting in equanimity, Moab, Utah, 2018.

Conclusion

PRAYER

Be My Guide

Be My Guide
O Lord, guide Thou my thoughts
Make them anchored in Thee.
Guide Thou my feelings
Purify them for love of Thee alone.
Guide Thou my actions
To be in service to Thee alone.
Guide Thou my words
Protecting Beauty, Truth, and Thy vibration.
O Lord, guide me always, move through me,
Make me a perfect Instrument of Divine Will.[7]

OM TAT SAT AUM

---

7   Yogacharya David, *Climbing the Sacred Mountain: Poems and Prayers of a Western Yogi* (p. 212).

References

Arnold, Edwin, Sir. (1905). *The Song Celestial or Bhagavad Gita*. London, England: Dryden House.

Hickenbottom, Yogacharya David. (2023). *Climbing the Sacred Mountain: Poems and Prayers of a Western Yogi. (2021)*. Camano Island, WA.: The Cross and the Lotus Publishing.

Hickenbottom, Yogacharya David. (2023). *Living a Spiritually Rich Life: Discourses Volume One: 2013–2014*. Camano Island, WA.: The Cross and the Lotus Publishing.

Hickenbottom, Yogacharya David. (2023). *Re-Union of Soul and Spirit: Discourses Volume Two: 2015*. Camano Island, WA.: The Cross and the Lotus Publishing.

Hickenbottom, Yogacharya David. (2023). *A True New Birth: Discourses Volume Three: 2016*. Camano Island, WA.: The Cross and the Lotus Publishing.

Hickenbottom, Yogacharya David. (2023). *Gateway to the Infinite: Discourses Volume Four: 2017*. Camano Island, WA.: The Cross and the Lotus Publishing.

Hickenbottom, Yogacharya David. (2023). *Standing on the Threshold of Eternity: Discourses Volume Five. 2018*. Camano Island, WA.: The Cross and the Lotus Publishing.

Hickenbottom, Yogacharya David. (2024). *Writing in the Book of Life: Discourses Volume Six. 2019*. Camano Island, WA.: The Cross and the Lotus Publishing.

Swami Sri Yukteswar. (1949/1963/1990). *The Holy Science.* Los Angeles, California: Self-Realization Fellowship.

Bible References

King James Bible Online:
https//www.kingjamesbibleonline.org

Website References

Yogacharya David's original discourse reference:
www.crossandlotus.com

Anandamayi reference: https://www.anandamayi.org

Anandashram reference: https://anandashram.org/

From the United States Declaration of Independence.
https://www.archives.gov

Image Attribution

All images are used courtesy of the David and Carla Hickenbottom portfolio. Photos were taken by David and Carla Hickenbottom or gifted with permission by friends, family, and devotees. Attribution for images from these sources has not been included here.

Acknowledgments

Yogacharya David has a unique ability to share spiritual teachings and soul-enhancing reflections in a most accessible manner—he can reach us in our day-to-day ways of being as we strive to live a purposeful life. He guides us, and even as he laughs at himself, he still seriously advocates for a wake-up process.

It is a privilege to form what we call Team-David, a small dedicated team of aspirants who willingly devote time and expertise to ensuring that Yogacharya David's legacy of teachings reaches those who long for a deeper, broader, disciplined-yet-freeing approach to life's journey.

Carla Hickenbottom, David's wife and senior disciple, has been a major support throughout the preparation and publication process. Her loving oversight and her diligence as director of The Cross and The Lotus Publishing support us each step of the way.

Rebecca Harvey has been a major ongoing link to data collection and historical document searches. She seems to know just where to find more information on most everything we need. Her keen eye also provides an astute read that catches the forever-escaping grammatical challenges. Charmie Gilcrease received 200 pages of quotes from me and lovingly took a year to theme them, brilliantly choosing to place Yogacharya David's words where she felt they best fit. It is a gift of Grace to have such a fine team working to prepare and publish Yogacharya David's legacy of teachings.

Jan Westendorp of Kato Design and Photo brings her artistic and professional book design expertise forward when working on our manuscripts. She provides us with elegant page layouts and image refinement support, and in so many other ways, she has helped us create a beautiful series of six volumes of Discourses, two volumes of quotes plus four other publications to date.

Of note, some of the quotes have minor grammar or word-placement changes in order to present a teaching in a succinct quote format.

Team-David feels that Yogacharya David would be delighted to know that his unique writings and teachings are available in book form for all who seek a deeper, sacred understanding of the human condition.

About the Author

Yogacharya David Hickenbottom (1954–2019) met his guru Yogacharya Mother Hamilton, a disciple of Paramhansa Yogananda, when he was a youth of 20. Mother Hamilton bestowed the Yogacharya title to David before she left her body in 1991.

The great Kriya Yoga lineage of India that came through Jesus, Babaji, Lahiri Mahasaya, and Sri Yukteswar to Yogananda, and then to Mother Hamilton, provides pathways to: an appreciation of, and a faith in, the everyday sacred, an understanding of higher dimensional wisdom, an integral intuitive knowing of spiritual truths, and the vibratory realms that permeate all that is, was, and will be.

Yogacharya David says: "An inner pain brought me to the path most unwillingly, and this inner pain kept me on the path. I put my shoulder to the wheel." He faced the crux of the spiritual dilemma—how to shift from the ego-driven lower or smaller human nature to a larger and luminous existence, intuitively attuned to our deeper and broader—vast—spiritual nature, thereby discovering the Living Truth. With this intense striving for Truth and Bliss, and with his Guru's Grace, David was carried through many years of Mystical Crucifixion spiritual experiences. His year in silence (2000–2001) established an inner state of stillness that never left him—and finally led him to his full Self-realization.

Also by Yogacharya David

Hickenbottom, Yogacharya David. (2024). *Resurrect the Listening Heart: Quotes Volume One.* Camano Island, WA.: The Cross and the Lotus Publishing.

Hickenbottom, Yogacharya David. (2025). *Seek the Sacred Code of the Universe: Quotes Volume Two.* Camano Island, WA.: The Cross and the Lotus Publishing.

2013–2019 Discourse Series: Published 2023–2024.

- *Discourses—Volume One: 2013–14: Living a Spiritually Rich Life*

- *Discourses—Volume Two: 2015: Re-Union of Soul and Spirit*

- *Discourses—Volume Three: 2016: A True New Birth*

- *Discourses—Volume Four: 2017: Gateway to the Infinite*

- *Discourses—Volume Five: 2018: Standing on the Threshold of Eternity*

- *Discourses—Volume Six: 2019: Writing in the Book of Life*

Hickenbottom, Yogacharya David. (2022). *Touching the Supreme Spirit*: Infinite Calendar. Camano Island, WA.: The Cross and The Lotus Publishing.

Hickenbottom, Yogacharya David. (2022). *Silence: Entering the Cosmic Sea of Consciousness*. Camano Island, WA.: The Cross and The Lotus Publishing.

Hickenbottom, Yogacharya David. (2022). *Notes to Sadhakas*. Camano Island, WA.: The Cross and The Lotus Publishing.

Hickenbottom, Yogacharya David. (2021). *Climbing the Sacred Mountain: Poems and Prayers of a Western Yogi*. Camano Island, WA.: The Cross and The Lotus Publishing.

Hickenbottom, Yogacharya David. (2019). *My Spiritual India*. Camano Island, WA.: The Cross and The Lotus Publishing.

. . . and more coming
Information on The Cross and The Lotus
can be found at
www.crossandlotus.com